# Makini's
# Vegan
# Kitchen

# Makini's
# Vegan Kitchen

### 10th Anniversary Edition
### of the *Plum* Cookbook

## MAKINI HOWELL

### Photographs by Charity Burggraaf

SASQUATCH BOOKS
SEATTLE

Printed in China

SASQUATCH BOOKS with colophon is a registered trademark of Penguin Random House LLC

27 26 25 24 23          9 8 7 6 5 4 3 2 1

Originally published as *Plum: Gratifying Vegan Dishes from Seattle's Plum Bistro* in hardcover in the United States by Sasquatch Books in 2013.

Editor: Susan Roxborough
Project editor: Michelle Hope Anderson | Copy editor: Diane Sepanski
Photographs: Charity Burggraaf | Cover photography: Elizabeth Rudge
Design: Anna Goldstein & Alison Keefe
Interior food styling: Julie Hopper | Cover food styling: Jenn Elliot Blake

Library of Congress Cataloging-in-Publication Data is available.

ISBN: 978-1-63217-457-4

Sasquatch Books
1325 Fourth Avenue, Suite 1025
Seattle, WA 98101

www.SasquatchBooks.com

FSC
www.fsc.org

MIX
Paper | Supporting
responsible forestry
FSC® C008047

**FOR MY PARENTS,** two people who caught a glimpse of the future of our food source and taught me how to inscribe it in cuisine

# Contents

# Recipe List

(**GF**)=Gluten Free, (**SF**)=Soy Free

## Fundamentals

Cream Cheese Crème Fraîche (**GF**) 3

Egg Foam and Green Egg Foam (**SF/GF**) 3

Green Egg Foam Water (**SF/GF**) 4

Sweet Soy Cream (**GF**) 4

Savory Soy Cream (**GF**) 6

Savory Rice Cream (**SF/GF**) 7

Sweet Rice Cream (**SF/GF**) 8

Basil Soy Ricotta (**GF**) 8

Agave Balsamic Vinaigrette (**SF/GF**) 9

Basil-Walnut Pesto (**SF/GF**) 9

Roasted Garlic Cloves Two Ways (**SF/GF**) 10

Raw Tofu Relish (**SF/GF**) 11

Garlic-Ginger Oil (**SF/GF**) 11

## Beginnings

Chocolate Crepes with Cream Cheese Crème Fraîche, Sliced Bananas, and Chocolate Maple Butter (**GF**) 14

Good Old-Fashioned Blueberry Pancakes (**SF/GF**) 15

Good Old-Fashioned French Toast Stuffed with Strawberries and Sweet Soy Cream 17

Tiramisu Pancakes 18

Fig Crepes with Ricotta, Arugula, and Agave Balsamic (**GF**) 19

Pesto Plum Pizza with Balsamic Arugula 21

Heirloom Tomato Toasts with Oregano, Grapes, and Ricotta Soy 22

Oyster Mushroom Scramble with Sweet Peppers, Onions, and Fresh Tofu (**GF**) 23

Savory French Toast "TLT" 24

## Salads and Soups

Grilled Black Plum and Jicama Salad with Radicchio (**GF**) 29

Quinoa-Millet Cherry Salad (**SF/GF**) 30

Polenta and Orange Salad with Fennel Salsa (**GF**) 32

Apple Ginger Salad (**SF/GF**) 35

Avocado Salad with Seitan Bites 36

Blood Orange and Fresh Tofu Salad (**GF**) 37

Roasted Beet and Blood Orange Salad with Cilantro Pesto (**SF/GF**) 38

Grilled Peach and Arugula Salad with Soy Ricotta and Grilled Sourdough Toast 40

Creamy Millet Corn Chowder (**SF/GF**) 41

Habanero Yam Soup (**GF**) 43

Cauliflower Bisque with Fresh Fennel (**GF**) 44

Raw Kale and Seaweed Salad with Fresh Tofu and Ginger-Garlic Oil (**GF**) 45

## Small Plates

Charred Broccolini (**SF/GF**) 49

Smashed Purple Potatoes with Parsley (**SF/GF**) 50

Chai-Spiced Yam Bruschetta with Crunchy Kale (**SF**) 52

Oven-Roasted Cherry Tomatoes with Thyme on Toast (**SF**) 53

Spicy Chili-Lime Edamame (**GF**) 55

Curried Red Yam Fries (**SF/GF**) 56

Grilled Wild Mushroom Toasts 58

Charred Brussels Sprouts and Fingerling Potatoes with Crispy Smoked Tofu (**GF**) 59

# Foreword

Foods can be magical, not just tasty, satisfying, and delicious—all the things we associate with a hearty meal. Foods can be so much more. They can transform your life.

At the Physicians Committee for Responsible Medicine, we have seen this in our research studies. People join our studies hoping to trim down, improve their health, or get off their medications. They learn to make healthier meals and are delighted to find that a menu change really does help them accomplish all these things. But when foods also boost their energy, dissolve long-standing aches and pains, and make them feel years younger, that's what many people have never had the chance to experience.

Magic can happen at a restaurant too. You come in from a busy Seattle street, looking for a bite to eat. With a friendly greeting, you're escorted to a table. As dinner is served, you discover this is no ordinary meal. The food is so delightfully prepared; so attractive, aromatic, and flavorful—familiar ingredients transformed into something you've never quite tasted before. And you understand exactly why Plum Bistro is so popular.

In this book, Makini Howell loans you her magic wand. She shows you the secrets she uses at Plum. Whether you are preparing a simple, quick meal or an elaborate dinner, these wonderful recipes are exactly what you are looking for.

As a doctor, I am always glad when patients improve their diets. The most important guarantee of their success is using ingredients and recipes that are appealing and tasty, so that they want to stick to their healthy resolve. The dishes at Plum go much, much further. They are so delightful, you'll want to come back again and again. And when dinner is this delightful, who would ever want to miss out on the magic?

**NEAL BARNARD, MD**
President, Physicians Committee for
Responsible Medicine, Washington, DC

# Introduction

It's been a minute. In the decade since I published this book, so much of life has happened. I still very much appreciate the art of food, and Plum Bistro has become all that I imagined it would be. We continue to tell a beautiful story of entrepreneurialism, family food, culture, and sustainability. Plum Bistro's journey has led me to *Makini's Vegan Kitchen*, which was originally published in hardcover as *Plum* a decade ago. It is a venture of the heart. Makini's Kitchen has now expanded into a vegan lifestyle brand with a tofu factory here in Georgetown, Seattle, manufacturing a tasty line of tofus in such flavors as Baba's Mesquite Tofu, Baba's Jerk Tofu, Baba's Tofustrami, and Baba's Taco Mix. You can order these in person or online for the recipes that call for them, or start your own plant-based traditions.

I started this brand to honor my dad, who the angels carried home in early 2021. To say my father's death was crushing does not come close to describing my feelings of loss. I did not want him to be forgotten; in fact, I want everyone to know how truly good a man he was. My father (we called him Baba) taught me how to cook, and he created all of the delicious and exciting flavors of our tofu we use in the restaurant, so I decided to share the goodness in his name.

A Plum Bistro cookbook came about through popular demand. So many of our customers ask how we do it, and oftentimes they're asking for more than just our recipes. Plum Bistro is about giving veganism a new definition, incorporating my generation's work ethics, beliefs, and style into what we do. We want our love of a plant-based diet to embody the change we're all going to meet in the coming years with regard to how we harvest food and how we treat our host planet.

Plum's food is honest and personal. It tells my story as a lifelong vegan, and it's made and served by a group of people who love the space they're in. They love preparing our food, as well as being a part of a small but influential community.

My intention with this book is to create a complete culinary experience. When I was in New York, even living in Brooklyn I was frustrated by the lack of vegan options. Eating out almost always meant having a salad. Although we do offer salads, at Plum there are no limits on being vegan. Instead, we like to think of what we do as an expansion—for me, vegan food is about flavor first. My recipes are shaped by traditions such as butter sauces, chimichurri dressing, and handmade pastas. I also use classic grilling techniques for everything from pizzas to vegetables. I'm really not trying to replace anything because I don't feel—and I've never felt—like I'm "missing" anything. I'm just using other sources of protein. What you'll find in these pages is a vegan reinterpretation of modern, smart, thoughtful food. You can cook our recipes easily at home, and we have a wide enough variety that you can revel in our dishes at every meal.

Our bistro reflects this same idea. When you step into Plum, whether you're a vegan or not, you won't miss a thing. Our food covers every meal and mood: we have a brunch menu, featuring Tiramisu Pancakes (page 18) and Good Old-Fashioned French Toast Stuffed with Strawberries and Sweet Soy Cream (page 17), among other treats. Happy-hour regulars line up for sage-infused gin-lemon cocktails served with our gourmet fries and dips and grilled pizzas. Families enjoy dinners of Hazelnut Tofu and Tempeh with Millet and Blueberry Salad (page 75), along with Spicy Peach Tofu and Tempeh with Charred Purple Beans (page 67). We've worked hard to expand the definition of what makes for a gratifying, innovative meal. Besides offering gluten- and nut-free dishes, we also have something called a transitional raw section on our menu. We want to be able to feed almost anyone.

This idea of changing the way you taste pushes us to experiment and recraft, to look at our dishes from outside the box and try to make them even tastier, more indulgent, and more vibrant. We unapologetically incorporate bold colors and spices to speak loudly to your culinary experience. One of our great passions is to draw on the simple traditions of American food to stir your palate and emotions. We are bright, daring, and sophisticated, and through our promise to do no harm to our animal neighbors, we peacefully extend to you all the bounty and beauty of the earth.

Our focus is to support local small and family-owned farms by using 90 percent regionally grown foods. Sometimes we use bananas, sure, and they don't grow in the Northwest, but we try to be conscious of when we're using foods from outside our region and why. We're also a 100 percent organic company.

This all-encompassing mindset comes naturally to me, because it's how I was raised. I was lucky enough to grow up completely vegan and organic with two entrepreneurial, truly progressive parents. My father, James Howell, inherited a grocery store that grew over the years into a family of restaurants, giving my siblings and me a business that has been in our family for years. And my folks fed us a completely plant-based diet that gave me the blueprint for Plum, for this book, and for the expansion of our green, sustainable, plant-based business.

In the 1980s, when the idea of a diet free of animal products was almost unheard of in the United States, my mother, Niombi, cut a swath through the natural food industry by demanding organics from all our purveyors. Long before "locavorism" was a concept, she deliberately developed relationships with certified organic tofu and tempeh companies within 360 miles of her businesses. She taught us how to farm in a backyard pea patch, and my folks created sauces and seasoning mixes that would be the foundation for a new way of experiencing the plant world.

My mother then created a tofu sandwich and a millet burrito—something completely unheard of at the time—and launched her sandwich company, Hillside Quickies vegan sandwiches. Her product line has been in every major co-op in the Seattle/Tacoma/Olympia area. She laid the blueprint for the vegan sandwich, all while home schooling and raising three mindful, vegan, organic kids.

I think of what we do at Plum as being a bridge, a space to create community. In fact, the name Plum represents a gathering space for all. It was inspired by the role of the plum tree in Japanese culture, where it symbolizes hope and community, constancy and kindness, the triumph of good over hardship. My hope was to create all of this in the restaurant, and I'm grateful to offer a place to celebrate and support all these values, whether I'm cooking on the line or greeting guests at the door.

*Makini's Vegan Kitchen*, formerly *Plum*, was born from my fortunate upbringing by vegan entrepreneurs—two people who had a vision of the future of food. The recipes here are just the beginning of my story. It's my sincere hope that this book not only builds on what my parents began, but that it also brings your newly vegan daughter, your gourmet son, and your skeptical in-laws—your whole family—to the table to celebrate *your* story.

# Fundamentals

A handful of recipes do multiple duty for us; they are versatile enough to use in everything from pancakes to pizza. When you start making Plum Bistro basics like Sweet Soy Cream (page 4) or Basil-Walnut Pesto (page 9), I bet they'll become staples in your kitchen too.

## A few notes that will help with all my recipes

I try to operate with as little waste as possible. I don't stem my kale, for instance, except to cut off any bruised bottoms (the stems are where most of the flavor is, too). Fresh herb stems go into my dishes right along with the leaves.

For all my rice and soy creams, I note that it's best to use a powerful blender, such as a Vitamix. But even an immersion blender will work, and you can also make them with a food processor, although the creams will come out a little thinner and slightly oilier that way.

Throughout the book, when I call for silken tofu I don't mean the smoothie silken tofu used in drinks. I'm talking about the firm silken tofu that is a type much like high-fiber tofu.

What is your favorite local small batch tofu or tempeh? Every community has a small place where you can buy handmade artisan tofu (and even sometimes tempeh) made in small batches. Buy that for any recipe calling for tofu or tempeh, or find Makini's Kitchen brand tofu. A local tofu tends to be more dense and have a fuller texture. A local tempeh will tend to have less of a strong tempeh flavor and it may be less dense and more nutty, especially sprouted tempeh.

# Cream Cheese Crème Fraîche (GF)

You can use crème fraîche in both savory and sweet dishes, and it makes a good substitute for Sweet Soy Cream (page 4). It will keep in the refrigerator for seven to ten days.

**Makes about 1¾ cups**

2 ounces (¼ cup) vegan cream cheese, softened

4 ounces soft tofu

½ teaspoon vanilla extract

¼ teaspoon ground cinnamon (optional)

1 cup canola oil

1 teaspoon white wine vinegar

In a blender, combine the cream cheese, tofu, vanilla, and cinnamon. With the machine running, slowly pour in the oil so it emulsifies and slightly thickens. Pour the mixture into a medium bowl, whisk in the vinegar, and continue whisking until the crème has the consistency of heavy cream.

# Egg Foam and Green Egg Foam (SF/GF)

When I first started using egg replacers, they didn't give me the effects I was after. They seemed gummy and didn't have the binding effect of real eggs. Tweaking the egg replacer into a foam gives you a fluffy mixture that can be used in most of the same ways you would use egg whites.

**Makes 1 cup**

2 tablespoons egg replacer (such as Ener-G brand)

1 cup room temperature water (if making Green Egg Foam, use Green Egg Foam Water; recipe follows)

Heat a burner to medium-high heat. Put the egg replacer and water in a large stainless-steel bowl. Placing the bowl directly on the burner, whisk the mixture until it starts to foam and thicken, about 2 minutes. (It will stick to the bottom if you don't whisk it continuously, so don't leave it unattended.) When the foam has fluffed up to about 1½ times its original size and its consistency is similar to that of a beaten egg, remove the bowl from the heat. (If you're not sure if the egg foam is done, you can measure it with an instant-read thermometer—its temperature should be about 100 degrees F at this point.) Though this egg foam will keep in the refrigerator for about twelve hours, it's best to use it as soon as possible because it will deflate over time.

# Green Egg Foam Water (SF/GF)

**Makes 1 cup**

4 cups spinach leaves, packed

½ cup room temperature water

Remember Green Eggs and Ham? Forget the ham, but do try this delicately green spinach version of egg foam, which is great for crepes and pastas. It's heavier than our standard foam but will have the same binding effect.

Heat a large pot of water to boiling. Boil the spinach leaves until they have wilted, about 15 to 30 seconds. Drain the leaves but do not squeeze out the excess water. You should have about ½ cup of wilted spinach.

Add the spinach and water to a blender and blend until smooth. Pour the mixture into a measuring cup and add enough room-temperature water to make 1 cup of liquid.

# Sweet Soy Cream (GF)

**Makes about 3 cups**

1 cup unsweetened soy milk

2 cups canola oil

1 tablespoon agave syrup

1¼ tablespoons freshly squeezed lemon juice

Vanilla extract, for sweetening (optional)

Ground cinnamon, for sweetening (optional)

This sweet version of our soy cream is a good substitute for whipped cream and crème fraîche. Like our savory version, it marries well with a variety of flavorings; try adding almond extract in place of the vanilla, ground cardamom in place of the cinnamon, or whatever else you can imagine.

Put the milk in a powerful blender, such as a Vitamix if you have one. (The more powerful the blender, the creamier the consistency of the final cream. You can use a food processor too, but the creams will come out thinner and a bit oilier.) With the machine running, drizzle in the oil very slowly, until it is thoroughly blended with the milk. Continue blending for another minute or so, until the mixture has the consistency of heavy cream. (Note that it will become more like a light whipped cream after you add the lemon juice.)

Pour the mixture into a medium bowl and whisk in the agave syrup, lemon juice, and vanilla and cinnamon to taste.

Store the cream in a tightly sealed jar in the refrigerator for up to a week. It will firm up to about the consistency of mayonnaise.

**BASIL SOY RICOTTA** (page 8)

**SWEET SOY CREAM** (page 4)

**RAW BASIL SOY RICOTTA** (page 8)

**CREAM CHEESE**
**CRÈME FRAÎCHE** (page 3)

# Savory Soy Cream (GF)

**Makes about 3 cups**

1 cup unsweetened soy milk

2 cups canola oil

1 to 1½ tablespoons apple cider vinegar

Minced garlic, for seasoning (optional)

This thick "cream" is something like a vegan mayonnaise. It's versatile enough to handle any number of flavorings, so feel free to play with seasonings other than the suggested garlic. If you have a soy-free diet, you can substitute Savory Rice Cream (page 7) in most recipes. For all vegan creams, make sure to add your oil quite slowly and stop when the mixture is the thickness you want, even if you haven't used up all the oil. The amount of vinegar you use will vary depending on how thick you want the cream to be.

___

Put the milk in a powerful blender, such as a Vitamix, if you have one. (The more powerful the blender, the creamier the consistency of the final cream.) With the machine running, drizzle in the oil very slowly, until it is thoroughly blended with the milk. Continue blending for another minute or so, until the mixture has the consistency of heavy cream. (Note that it will become more like a light whipped cream after you add the vinegar.)

Pour the mixture into a medium bowl and whisk in the vinegar and garlic to taste.

Store the cream in a tightly sealed jar in the refrigerator for up to a week. It will firm up to about the consistency of mayonnaise. Re-whip it with a whisk to return it to its original texture, adding a little more milk if need be.

# Savory Rice Cream (SF/GF)

This base cream has all the versatility of our Savory Soy Cream (page 6) but with the advantage of being soy- and gluten-free. It's runnier than the soy cream, about the consistency of a thin sour cream. You can add flavorings such as garlic or herbs, or substitute other milks (nut, hemp, oat) or oils (peanut, soy, sunflower) as you like for your dietary needs.

Xanthan gum is a gluten-free thickener that can be found in most major supermarkets or online through sources such as Bob's Red Mill (BobsRedMill.com).

Put the milk, xanthan gum, and lemon juice (or more juice to taste) in a blender. (You could use a food processor as well, but the cream will be thinner and a bit oilier.) Mix on high speed until frothy. With the machine running, slowly drizzle in the oil until the mixture is slightly thickened and creamy. You can store the cream in a tightly sealed jar in the refrigerator for 5 to 7 days

**Makes about 2 cups**

1 cup cold unsweetened rice milk

1 teaspoon xanthan gum*

2 tablespoons freshly squeezed lemon juice (from 1 medium lemon)

¾ cup canola oil

**\*NOTE:** Add another ¼ teaspoon to ½ teaspoon xanthan gum if you want a thicker consistency, keeping in mind that the cream will thicken more after it's refrigerated. The more gum you add, the more gelatin-like the texture will become.

# Sweet Rice Cream (SF/GF)

Many of our customers think soy is all they can eat if they're going to be vegans. I wanted to develop a rich cream that would be a good alternative to that—it's also gluten-free, so it's great for people with celiac disease as well as soy allergies. It's a little thinner than dairy creams, but it's really tasty.

---

Put the milk, sugar, xanthan gum, and lemon juice (or more juice to taste) in a blender. (You can use a food processor, but the cream will be thinner and a bit oilier.) Mix on high speed until frothy. With the machine running, slowly drizzle in the oil until the mixture is slightly thickened and creamy. (It will thicken more after it's refrigerated.) You can store the cream in a tightly sealed jar in the refrigerator for 5 to 7 days.

**Makes about 2 cups**

1 cup cold unsweetened rice milk

1 teaspoon sugar

1 teaspoon xanthan gum*

2 tablespoons freshly squeezed lemon juice (from 1 medium lemon)

¾ cup canola oil

**\*NOTE:** Add another ¼ teaspoon to ½ teaspoon xanthan gum if you want a thicker consistency, keeping in mind that the cream will thicken more after it's refrigerated. The more gum you add, the more gelatin-like the texture will become.

# Basil Soy Ricotta (GF)

The trick to this recipe is using a mild-flavored, firm silken tofu and draining it completely. This will give you a sturdy, creamy ricotta that, when cooked, takes on a slightly crumbly texture. If you use a blender instead of a food processor, make the ricotta in two batches so it doesn't get overworked.

---

Put the tofu, dried basil, garlic, salt, pepper, oil, cane juice, and lemon juice (or more lemon juice to taste) in a blender or the bowl of a food processor. Blend in short bursts until the mixture is smooth, about 3 to 5 minutes. Add the fresh basil and continue blending until it's thoroughly incorporated and the mixture is creamy, about 15 to 20 seconds. It will keep in the refrigerator for 7 to 10 days.

**Makes about 2½ cups**

2 pounds silken firm or regular tofu (preferably your favorite local brand)

1 teaspoon dried basil

½ teaspoon chopped garlic

1 teaspoon sea salt

1 teaspoon freshly ground pepper

¼ cup olive oil

2 teaspoons evaporated cane juice

2½ tablespoons freshly squeezed lemon juice (from 1 medium lemon)

2 tablespoons chopped fresh basil leaves (about 5 large)

# Agave Balsamic Vinaigrette (SF/GF)

This sweet-tart dressing can be made in a flash. A clean, empty salad-dressing bottle works well.

Combine all the ingredients in a container with a tight-fitting lid. Cover tightly and shake well to blend.

**Makes about ⅔ cup**

¼ cup balsamic vinegar, preferably an aged variety

⅓ cup olive oil

2 tablespoons agave syrup

½ teaspoon sea salt

½ teaspoon freshly ground pepper

1 tablespoon fresh basil, chopped

¼ teaspoon chopped garlic (optional)

# Basil-Walnut Pesto (SF/GF)

Every time I go somewhere and want to order a pesto dish, it has cheese in it. Pestos are great, and they should be vegan too. When I was trying to figure out what created that characteristic taste and consistency, I realized I could replace the cheese with nuts. What you get is a dairy-free, soy-free, gluten-free spread that has so many uses—try it on sandwiches, with salads, or, as we do here (page 73) with tofu.

Put all the ingredients in a blender or the bowl of a food processor. Puree until smooth, about 15 seconds.

**Makes about 1 ½ cups**

1½ ounces fresh basil leaves and stems, roughly chopped (about 1 cup)

¼ cup olive oil

1 teaspoon freshly squeezed lemon juice

½ teaspoon chopped garlic

½ cup loosely packed baby arugula, tough stems discarded

¼ teaspoon sea salt

¼ teaspoon freshly ground pepper

2 tablespoons walnut pieces

# Roasted Garlic Cloves Two Ways

**Makes ½ cup**

On the stovetop:

1 head of garlic cloves, peeled and washed

1 cup canola oil

In the oven:

1 head garlic

Canola oil, for coating the garlic

Most recipes for roasted garlic cloves tell you to bake the oiled head of garlic in an oven. To me, that way turns the garlic into a mushy paste that's hard to get out of the cloves. It didn't work for what I wanted—real pieces of garlic to use as a condiment.

Put these on pizzas or add them to pastas or anywhere you need an added punch. The oil is as useful a flavor booster as the cloves.

Many people don't call for washing cloves after peeling them, but the way I learned to cook was to wash all fruits and vegetables.

---

**ON THE STOVETOP:**

Heat the garlic and oil together in a heavy-bottomed medium saucepan over medium-low heat, stirring occasionally. Cook for about 10 to 15 minutes, taking care not to burn the cloves (if they appear in danger of burning, lower the heat). When the cloves have softened and just turned golden brown, remove the pan from the heat and let them cool in the oil. They will continue to cook and soften further as they cool. Once the garlic is cool, store it in a glass bottle with the oil so that the flavors continue to marry. Use it in dishes such as Blue Corn Pizza with Pesto-Grilled Heirloom Tomatoes and Ricotta (page 108).

**IN THE OVEN:**

Preheat the oven to 400 degrees F.

Slice off and discard about ¼ inch from the top of the garlic head to expose the individual cloves. Coat the head generously with oil, wrap it in aluminum foil, and place it in a small baking dish. Roast the garlic until the cloves are soft and browned, about 30 minutes. Let the head cool, then squeeze it to pop out the individual cloves.

# Raw Tofu Relish (SF/GF)

I actually developed this recipe after watching one of my prep cooks make our ricotta tofu the wrong way. Instead of correcting him, I realized "I could make that into a relish." We use it to top pizzas and as a garnish. It's especially good for people looking for a topping that doesn't have a creamy texture. What a happy accident!

---

Crumble the tofu into bead-size pieces in a medium bowl. Add the fresh and dried basil, garlic, salt, pepper, oil, cane juice, and lemon juice (or more lemon juice to taste), and mix well.

**Makes about 2 cups**

2 pounds silken firm or regular tofu (preferably your favorite local brand)l

¼ cup fresh basil leaves, cut into ribbons

½ teaspoon dried basil

1 teaspoon minced garlic

1 teaspoon sea salt

1 teaspoon freshly ground pepper

¼ cup olive oil

2 teaspoons evaporated cane juice

2 tablespoons freshly squeezed lemon juice (from 1 medium lemon)

# Garlic-Ginger Oil (SF/GF)

Ginger doesn't always have to give dishes an Asian influence. With this oil, it can take food in almost any direction you want. Think of it as a base for dressings or a way to add layers of flavor to foods. Put in some lime, salt, and pepper and it'll make a good salad dressing. Pour it over edamame for a twist. Add it to mashed yams. Use the bits of garlic and ginger in it to bring in a little spice.

---

In a large sauté pan, heat the oil over medium-low heat. Add the garlic and ginger and cook until they just start to brown, 5 to 7 minutes (they will continue to cook as the oil cools). Remove the pan from the heat and let the oil cool before transferring it to a covered container. It will keep in the refrigerator for 2 to 3 weeks.

**Makes 1½ cups**

1 cup canola oil

¼ cup garlic cloves, peeled and washed (from about ½ medium head of garlic)

¼ cup chopped peeled fresh ginger (from about a 2-inch piece)

# Beginnings

Plum's brunch customers are always happily surprised to see all their traditional favorites on our menu, from French toast and pancakes to crepes and scrambles. How do we do it? We rely on the same fundamentals—milk, butter, and eggs—but we work with soy or rice milk instead of cow's milk, and use vegan versions of butter and cream that are fairly interchangeable with those from animals. Eggs were trickier to figure out, but we found a way to tweak store-bought egg replacers into a billowy foam that binds our batters and lets us enjoy almost any morning treat.

# Chocolate Crepes with Cream Cheese Crème Fraîche, Sliced Bananas, and Chocolate Maple Butter (GF)

**Makes 4 servings**

For the crepes:

1 cup unsweetened soy milk

⅓ cup water

⅓ cup Egg Foam (recipe page 3)

2 tablespoons vegan buttery spread (such as Earth Balance brand), melted

¾ cup all-purpose gluten-free flour

¾ cup unsweetened cocoa powder

¼ cup sifted powdered sugar

Vegetable oil cooking spray

For the chocolate maple butter:

¼ cup (½ stick) vegan buttery spread (such as Earth Balance brand)

½ cup maple syrup

¼ cup vegan chocolate syrup (such as Santa Cruz Organic brand)

For garnish:

½ cup Cream Cheese Crème Fraîche (recipe page 3)

2 bananas, sliced

Confectioners' sugar, for dusting (optional)

Many brands of high-quality dark chocolate are naturally dairy-free, as are many cocoa powders and chocolate syrups. I like to flavor and color these crepes with cocoa powder and gild them with chocolate maple butter because I think it's hard to have too much chocolate on one plate.

---

To make the crepes, whisk the soy milk, water, and egg foam in a medium bowl, then add the buttery spread and mix together. In a separate large bowl, whisk together the flour, cocoa powder, and powdered sugar. Whisk the wet ingredients into the dry ingredients until smooth.

Spray a small crepe pan or frying pan with cooking spray and heat over medium heat. Coat the bottom with a thin layer of crepe batter. Cook for about 1 minute, until the crepe starts to bubble in the middle and turns opaque. Loosen the edges with a soft spatula, then flip the crepe and cook for 1 more minute on the other side, until the edges look crisp. If you prefer a drier crepe, cook for 1 or 2 minutes longer. Remove the crepe and repeat with the remaining batter.

If you are serving all the crepes together, preheat the oven to 200 degrees F. Warm the crepes in a single layer on 2 large baking sheets until ready to serve.

To make the chocolate maple butter, melt the buttery spread in a small saucepan over medium-low heat. Add the maple and chocolate syrups. Mix thoroughly and heat until warmed through. Keep warm over low heat.

To serve, layer 4 crepes in triangles on each plate, spooning a few tablespoons of the chocolate maple butter between each layer. Top each stack with 2 tablespoons of the crème fraîche and a handful of banana slices. Dust with the confectioners' sugar.

# Good Old-Fashioned Blueberry Pancakes (SF/GF)

Not that long ago, going gluten-free meant either avoiding baked goods outright or piecing together a workable mix from different bags of acceptable dry goods, such as rice flour or teff. Now manufacturers such as King Arthur Flour and Bob's Red Mill have done all the blending in the correct proportions, and their gluten-free all-purpose flours are available at major markets. A small company called Authentic Foods (AuthenticFoods.com) has a gluten- and soy-free blend I like that includes xanthan gum and cornstarch, which makes a texture I prefer. These gluten- and soy-free blueberry pancakes are as fluffy as the classic ones.

---

In a large bowl, sift together the flour, baking powder, baking soda, salt, and sugar. In a small bowl, whisk together the milk and oil. Make a well in the center of the dry ingredients and pour the wet ingredients into it. Using a wooden spoon, gently mix the ingredients (don't whip them until smooth; lumps are good here) and set the batter aside to rest for 5 minutes. After the batter has rested, fold in the blueberries.

If you'll be serving the pancakes all at once, preheat the oven to 200 degrees F. Warm the pancakes in a single layer on 2 large baking sheets until you're ready to serve them.

Lightly oil a griddle or medium frying pan and heat over medium-high heat. Using a small ladle or scoop and working in batches, pour about ¼ cup of batter onto the griddle for each pancake. Cook for 1½ to 2 minutes until bubbles form in the center, then flip the pancakes with a spatula. Cook on the other side until the bottoms are lightly browned, another 1 to 2 minutes. Remove the pancakes, either to a plate or a baking sheet, and repeat with the remaining batter, adding more oil to the griddle as necessary. Serve topped with the maple syrup and buttery spread.

**Makes 1 dozen 3-inch pancakes (4 servings)**

1½ cups gluten-free all-purpose flour

1 tablespoon baking powder

1½ teaspoons baking soda

½ teaspoon sea salt

2 teaspoons sugar

1¼ cups almond milk

2 tablespoons canola oil, plus extra for oiling the griddle

1 cup fresh blueberries

Maple syrup and vegan buttery spread (such as Earth Balance brand), for serving

# Good Old-Fashioned French Toast Stuffed with Strawberries and Sweet Soy Cream

This luxurious stuffed French toast is the classic model, creamy and sweet. I like making it with soft potato bread, which absorbs the liquid quickly. Rustic loaves also taste great but will have a firmer texture. Adjust the fruit depending on the season—think of strawberries in early summer, figs in the fall. The French toast can be made ahead of time, wrapped in individual slices, and frozen for up to a week.

In a medium bowl, whisk the milk and vinegar until the mixture thickens. Add the foam, vanilla, agave syrup, and cinnamon (or more cinnamon to taste), and whisk to combine. Set aside.

If you'll be serving the French toast all at once, preheat the oven to 200 degrees F. Warm the slices in a single layer on 2 large baking sheets until you're ready to serve them.

Lightly oil a griddle or large frying pan and heat over medium-high heat. Halve each bread slice nearly to the bottom, leaving the bread attached at the spine like an open book. Working in batches, dip the bread into the milk mixture for about 30 seconds on each side, then place on the griddle. Cook the bread until it turns golden brown, 4 to 7 minutes, then flip it with a spatula. Cook it on the other side until the bottom is crisp and browned, about 4 more minutes. Remove the bread, either to a plate or a baking sheet, and repeat with the remaining slices, adding more oil to the griddle as necessary.

To serve, spoon ¼ cup strawberries onto the bottom half of each piece of French toast. Fold the top over, add a dollop of the cream, and drizzle with the sorghum syrup. Serve immediately.

**Makes 4 servings**

1½ cups vanilla soy milk

1 teaspoon white vinegar

1 cup Egg Foam (page 3)

1½ teaspoons vanilla extract

1 teaspoon agave syrup

½ teaspoon ground cinnamon

¼ cup canola oil, plus extra for oiling the griddle

4 slices bread, about 2 inches thick by 4 inches long

1 cup hulled, sliced fresh strawberries

½ cup Sweet Soy Cream (page 4)

Sorghum syrup, for drizzling on French toast

# Tiramisu Pancakes

**Makes about 1 dozen 3-inch pancakes (4 servings)**

For the cream:

2 ounces (¼ cup) vegan cream cheese, softened

8 ounces silken firm tofu, crumbled

2 tablespoons coffee liqueur

2 tablespoons maple syrup

1 tablespoon white vinegar

For the pancakes:

1¾ cups unsweetened soy milk, divided

1 teaspoon white vinegar

½ cup vegan sour cream

¼ cup (½ stick) vegan buttery spread (such as Earth Balance brand), melted

2 teaspoons vanilla extract

2 tablespoons very finely ground coffee

2 cups all-purpose flour

2 tablespoons sugar

2 rounded tablespoons unsweetened cocoa powder

2 teaspoons baking powder

½ teaspoon baking soda

Generous pinch of sea salt

Canola oil, for oiling the griddle

½ cup maple syrup

1 teaspoon ground cinnamon

¼ cup vegan chocolate syrup (such as Santa Cruz Organic brand), for drizzling on pancakes

Plain pancakes are fine for breakfast, but sometimes a Sunday brunch calls for a special treat. Our popular Tiramisu Pancakes play off the classic Italian layered dessert. They're sophisticated and grown-up, with a splash of coffee liqueur and all the original's creamy, lush flavors intact.

To make the cream, put the cream cheese, tofu, liqueur, and maple syrup in a blender or food processor and puree just until smooth. Whisk in the vinegar and let the cream sit while you make the pancakes; it will thicken slightly.

To make the pancakes, first you'll need to make a thickened soy milk, which has the texture of buttermilk and lightens the cakes. Pour ¼ cup of the milk into a small bowl and whisk in the vinegar. Let the mixture sit for 1 to 2 minutes until thickened. Don't make it in advance; it's best fresh.

In a medium bowl, combine the thickened soy milk, the remaining 1½ cups milk, sour cream, buttery spread, vanilla, and coffee. Whisk until smooth. In a large bowl, sift together the flour, sugar, cocoa powder, baking powder, baking soda, and salt. Make a well in the center of the dry ingredients and pour the wet ingredients into it. Using a wooden spoon, gently mix the ingredients together. Don't whip the mixture; lumps are good here. Set the batter aside to rest for 5 minutes.

If you'll be serving the pancakes all at once, preheat the oven to 200 degrees F. Warm the pancakes in a single layer on 2 large baking sheets until you're ready to serve.

Lightly oil a griddle or medium frying pan and heat over medium-high heat. Using a small ladle or scoop and working in batches, pour about ¼ cup of batter onto the griddle for each pancake. Cook for 1 to 2 minutes until bubbles start to form in the center, then flip the pancakes with a spatula. Cook on the other side until the bottoms are lightly browned, another 1 to 2 minutes. Remove the pancakes, either to a plate or a baking sheet, and repeat with the remaining batter, adding more oil to the griddle as necessary.

To serve, stack a few pancakes on each plate, spreading a few tablespoons of cream between each layer. Drizzle the top of each stack with maple syrup and chocolate syrup, and sprinkle with a pinch of cinnamon.

# Fig Crepes with Ricotta, Arugula, and Agave Balsamic (GF)

Make these savory, filling crepes in the early fall when fresh figs are plump and soft and rich. I stuff the crepes with Basil Soy Ricotta (page 8) so they're almost like a breakfast version of manicotti. If you don't want them to be gluten-free, just use regular all-purpose flour.

Whisk the foam and milk in a medium bowl, then add the buttery spread and whisk until combined. In a large bowl, whisk together the flour and sugar. Add the wet ingredients to the dry ingredients and whisk until just combined.

If you'll be serving the crepes all at once, preheat the oven to 200 degrees F. Warm the crepes in a single layer on 2 large baking sheets until you're ready to serve.

Spray a small crepe pan or frying pan with the cooking oil and heat over medium-high heat. Coat the bottom of the pan with a thin layer of crepe batter, using about ¼ cup. Cook for about 1 minute, until the crepe starts to bubble in the middle and turns opaque. Loosen the edges with a soft spatula, then flip the crepe and cook for 1 minute more on the other side, until the edges are crisp while the middle is still soft. If you prefer a drier crepe, cook for 1 to 2 minutes longer. Remove the crepe, either to a plate or a baking sheet, and repeat with the remaining batter.

To serve, spoon 2 tablespoons of the ricotta down the center of each crepe, then, starting from one edge, loosely roll up the crepes. Put the figs and arugula in a small bowl and toss with the vinaigrette. Place 2 rolled crepes seam-side down on each of 6 serving plates and top with about ¼ cup of dressed fig salad.

**Makes 1 dozen 6-inch crepes (6 servings)**

⅓ cup Egg Foam (page 3)

1⅓ cups unsweetened soy milk

2 tablespoons vegan buttery spread (such as Earth Balance brand), melted

1 cup gluten-free all-purpose flour

2 tablespoons sugar

Canola oil cooking spray, for coating the pan

1½ cups Basil Soy Ricotta (page 8)

8 medium fresh figs, quartered

1 cup arugula or mixed greens, tough stems discarded

2 teaspoons Agave Balsamic Vinaigrette (page 9)

# Pesto Plum Pizza with Balsamic Arugula

In this fresh, light recipe, pizza makes surprisingly good brunch food. It may be topped with fruit, but don't mistake it for dessert; plums are more sweet-tart than candy-like. They make this dish even more of a main event when combined with the contrasting flavors of bitter greens, nutty pesto, and basil ricotta.

---

Preheat the oven to 450 degrees F.

Prebake the pizza crust on a pizza stone until it's firm and easy to move from the oven but is not browned, about 5 to 7 minutes (or estimate from package instructions).

Remove the crust from the oven, spread the pesto evenly over the top, then add the ricotta in evenly spaced dollops. Return the pizza to the oven and bake for another 10 minutes, until the edges are golden brown.

In a small bowl, toss the arugula and plum slices with the vinaigrette.

Remove the pizza from the oven, scatter the dressed plum salad over it, slice, and serve immediately.

**Makes one 9-inch pizza**

1 store-bought 9-inch pizza crust

⅓ cup Basil-Walnut Pesto (page 9)

⅓ cup Basil Soy Ricotta (page 8)

⅓ cup arugula, tough stems discarded

1 medium plum, cut into ¼-inch wedges

1 tablespoon Agave Balsamic Vinaigrette (page 9)

# Heirloom Tomato Toasts with Oregano, Grapes, and Ricotta Soy

**Makes 8 toasts (4 servings)**

3 to 4 small heirloom tomatoes

1 tablespoon whole fresh oregano leaves

4 Roasted Garlic Cloves (page 10), sliced

1 tablespoon Rosemary-Infused Olive Oil (recipe follows)

Sea salt and freshly ground pepper

8 slices bread

3 tablespoons Basil Soy Ricotta (page 8), more if using large bread slices

8 grapes (any variety), halved

**Makes 1 cup**

2 sprigs fresh rosemary, 5 to 6 inches long

1 cup good-quality extra-virgin olive oil

3 Roasted Garlic Cloves (page 10)

The key to this dish isn't necessarily the tomatoes—it's hard to go wrong with fresh heirlooms in season. The trickier part is the bread you choose for the toast. You need a loaf that's sturdy enough to stand up to the ricotta and tomatoes instead of being overwhelmed by their flavors and weight. I like to use a crusty sourdough baguette or thick potato bread.

---

Slice the tomatoes ¼ inch thick. Halve any slices that are otherwise too large to fit on the bread. In a large bowl, toss the tomatoes with the oregano, garlic, and oil (or more oil to taste), and season to taste with salt and pepper. Toast or grill the bread and spread each slice with ricotta. Arrange a few pieces of tomato on each slice, covering about ¾ of the bread and making sure each includes garlic and oregano. Arrange the grape halves decoratively over each slice.

## Rosemary-Infused Olive Oil

Dipping rosemary sprigs into boiling water intensifies their flavor during the infusion process. It's best to make the oil a week or so before you plan on using it to let the flavors develop.

---

Bring a small saucepan of water to a boil. Dip the rosemary sprigs in the boiling water and swirl them around for a few seconds, then remove. Pat them with paper towels until completely dry.

If the oil is not already at room temperature, heat the oil in a small saucepan over low heat until it's just warm, 1 to 2 minutes. Remove the pan from the heat and let the oil cool for 5 to 7 minutes.

Put the garlic and rosemary sprigs in a clean, dry glass bottle. Pour the oil over them. Let the bottle cool to room temperature, then seal it with a cork or tight-fitting lid. It will keep, stored in a cool, dry place, for 7 days, or in the refrigerator for about 2 weeks. If it gets cloudy when refrigerated, you can clear it by warming it to room temperature.

# Oyster Mushroom Scramble with Sweet Peppers, Onions, and Fresh Tofu (GF)

Oyster mushrooms lend themselves well to scrambles; they boast a meaty texture but an accommodatingly mild flavor. The texture of crumbled silken tofu here is a lot like scrambled eggs, while snippets of fresh herbs bring the flavors alive in a way that dried herbs can't duplicate.

Heat the oil in a large sauté pan over medium-high heat. Add the garlic (or more to taste) and cook until it starts to brown, 1 to 2 minutes. Add the mushrooms and toss them in the pan for about 30 seconds, coating them in the garlic. Add the onions and bell peppers and cook for a few minutes more, until they begin to soften. Crumble the tofu with your hands directly into the pan. Cook it for about 2 minutes, stirring with a soft spatula to avoid crushing it—this will give you a scrambled egg–like texture; cook it longer if you prefer a firmer consistency. Stir in the basil, parsley, tamari (or more tamari to taste), and red pepper flakes, and season to taste with salt and pepper. Cook for an additional minute, until the herbs begin to wilt. Remove from the heat and serve.

**Makes 4 servings**

1 tablespoon canola or other neutral oil

2 teaspoons chopped garlic

8 ounces oyster mushrooms, cleaned and separated

½ sweet yellow onion, cut into ¼-inch matchsticks (about ½ cup)

½ medium red bell pepper, cut into ¼-by-2-inch matchsticks (about ½ cup)

1 (14- to 16-ounce) package firm silken tofu (particularly a local, small-batch brand of tofu)

¼ cup loosely packed chopped fresh basil leaves

1 scant tablespoon chopped fresh parsley

1 tablespoon gluten-free tamari

Pinch of crushed red pepper flakes

Sea salt and freshly ground pepper

*NOTE: Silken tofu is a type of tofu much like high fiber or traditional firm. Everywhere silken is used in this book, it indicates a silken firm tofu, not a smooth soft silken version of tofu.

# Savory French Toast "TLT"

**Makes 8 pieces (4 servings)**

¼ cup canola oil

8 ounces firm smoked tofu (such as Baba's Mesquite Tofu), cut into 24 very thin slices of ⅛ inch or less

1½ cups unsweetened soy milk

½ teaspoon white wine vinegar

1 cup Egg Foam (page 3)

Sea salt and freshly ground pepper

Pinch of crushed red pepper flakes

2 teaspoons chopped fresh dill

8 pieces rustic bread, cut into slices about 1 inch thick by 4 inches wide by 5 inches long

½ cup Lemon Dill Aioli (recipe follows)

2 cups mixed spring greens or baby spinach

2 medium tomatoes, cut into 16 very thin slices

1 avocado, peeled, pitted, and thinly sliced, for garnish

Never mind the BLT. Smoked tofu makes for a gooooooood with a capital G savory French toast sandwich that also takes advantage of fresh veggies and herby aioli. We sell our own Makini's Kitchen brand tofu called Baba's Mesquite Tofu, and I recommend laying in some for this recipe if it's available in your region. If you're buying a national brand, look for a firm smoked tofu (or, in a pinch, seasoned tofu) that can be cut thin without crumbling. Ripe tomatoes, ideally flavor-rich heirlooms, make this shine.

---

Heat the oil in a large skillet over medium-high heat. Add the tofu slices in batches and fry until they crisp like bacon, 1 minute or so on each side. Using a slotted spatula, remove the tofu to a paper towel–lined plate, but keep the flavored oil in the skillet to fry the French toast.

In a medium bowl, whisk the milk and vinegar together until the mixture thickens. Whisk in the egg foam. Season to taste with salt and pepper, and mix in the red pepper flakes and dill.

If you'll be serving the French toast all at once, preheat the oven to 200 degrees F. Warm the slices in a single layer on 2 large baking sheets until you're ready to serve.

Lower the heat under the skillet to medium. Working in batches, dip the bread into the milk mixture for about 30 seconds on each side, then place it in the skillet. Cook the bread until it turns golden brown, 4 to 7 minutes, then flip it with a spatula. Cook it on the other side until the bottom is crisp and browned, about 4 more minutes. Remove the French toast, either to a plate or a baking sheet, and repeat with the remaining slices.

To serve, spread each piece of French toast with about 1 tablespoon of aioli. Pile about ¼ cup of greens on top, then layer with 3 slices of cooked tofu and 2 tomato slices. Garnish each with a slice of avocado and serve open-faced.

# Lemon Dill Aioli

Put the dill, lemon juice, garlic, salt, pepper, and soy cream in a blender or the bowl of a food processor and blend until well incorporated. To make a looser sauce rather than the firmer aioli, whisk in the milk and add an extra pinch of salt and pepper.

**Makes about 2 ¼ cups**

1 tablespoon finely minced fresh dill

Juice of 1 medium lemon

6 Roasted Garlic Cloves (page 10)

2 teaspoons sea salt

2 teaspoons freshly ground pepper

2 cups Savory Soy Cream (page 6) or store-bought vegan mayonnaise (such as Vegenaise brand)

¼ cup unsweetened soy milk (optional)

**NOTE:** To make this soy-free, substitute Savory Rice Cream (page 8) for the soy cream.

# Salads and Soups

I set the bar high with my salads and soups. They're such traditional fallback meals for vegan guests, and they're so often boring or bland. To meet my standards, they need to shout out something special, with vibrant colors, punchy flavors, and exciting ingredients.

# Grilled Black Plum and Jicama Salad with Radicchio (GF)

I like this sharp-sweet salad in the shoulder season when late summer gives way to early fall. Delectable, tart plums are at their best as the summer ends, while rich, bitter radicchio is just starting to come into its own. The ricotta helps tie their flavors together, while jicama gives the dish a nice layer of crunch.

To make the salad, heat the oil in a medium skillet over medium-high heat. Add the ricotta and cook for 5 to 10 minutes, stirring occasionally, until it browns on the bottom and acquires a drier texture. Set aside.

Preheat a stovetop or outdoor gas grill for 5 minutes on high heat.

Sprinkle the salt and pepper evenly over the cut side of the plums, both the edges and inside cavity. If using an outdoor grill, oil the grate so the plum skins don't stick. Grill the plums for 2 to 3 minutes on each side, until distinct grill marks form. Remove the plums to a plate and set aside.

Zest the limes, taking care to avoid the bitter pith, then juice them, reserving the juice for the dressing. (You'll need 4 teaspoons of zest and ¼ cup juice.) Put the radicchio, lettuce, jicama, lime zest, and chilies into a large bowl and toss gently. Set aside while you make the dressing.

To make the dressing, whisk the oil, reserved lime juice, agave syrup, salt, and pepper in a medium bowl.

To serve, divide the salad among 4 plates. Arrange 2 plum halves on top of the salad on each plate. Drizzle the dressing over the salad and sprinkle the ricotta on top.

**Makes 4 servings**

For the salad:

1 tablespoon canola oil

1 cup Basil Soy Ricotta (page 8)

Sea salt and freshly ground pepper

4 medium plums (about ¾ pound), halved and pitted

2 large limes

1 large head radicchio, torn into bite-size pieces

1 small head butter lettuce, torn into bite-size pieces

8 ounces jicama, peeled and cut into ¼-inch matchsticks (about 1 cup)

4 serrano chilies, seeded and thinly sliced

For the dressing:

2 tablespoons olive oil

2 tablespoons agave syrup

½ teaspoon sea salt

½ teaspoon freshly ground pepper

# Quinoa-Millet Cherry Salad (SF/GF)

**Makes 4 servings**

½ cup millet

½ cup quinoa

¼ cup almonds

8 ounces fresh cherries, pitted and cut in a mix of halves and quarters (I like a mix of red and yellow varieties)

½ small red onion, finely chopped

1 small jalapeño, seeded and minced

Juice of 1 medium lime

¼ cup fresh cilantro, stemmed and leaves coarsely chopped

3 to 4 mint leaves, cut into thin ribbons, for garnish

This amazing gluten-free, soy-free, and protein-packed salad is a fun way to use one of the fruits that signals when spring has finally arrived in rainy Seattle. When I was a little girl, we had a cherry tree in our backyard, and I couldn't wait for summer to come so I could climb the tree and gather all the cherries my pockets could hold. Now I'm all grown up and sated enough with red Bings and yellow Rainiers and even sour pie–candidates like the Montmorency to consider dressing them up a little.

This salad is very versatile. It's equally delicious served hot or cold. If you don't have both grains, it's still perfect with just one. And if you'd like an added kick, toss the toasted almonds with a pinch of smoked paprika.

---

Mix the millet and quinoa in a large bowl. Rinse the grains several times under running water, rubbing them together with your fingers, until the water stops foaming and runs clear.

To cook the grains to the texture I think is ideal, where they won't stick together, put 6 cups of water in a large saucepan. Add the grains, bring the water to a boil, and cook until the millet softens and the quinoa pops and forms little tails at the end, about 15 to 20 minutes. Pour the cooked grains through a strainer, being very careful that the hot water doesn't burn you; there may be about a cup of water remaining. Or, bring 2 cups of water to a boil in a medium saucepan. Add the grains, lower the heat to a simmer, and cook until all the water is absorbed and the grains are tender enough to fluff with a fork, about 15 to 20 minutes. If you'll be serving the salad cold, chill the grains in the refrigerator until you're ready to use them.

Heat a small dry skillet over medium-low heat. Put in the almonds and toast for a few minutes, tossing or stirring frequently, until the nuts are fragrant and lightly browned. Let the almonds cool before using.

When the almonds are cool enough to handle, coarsely chop them and put them in a large bowl, along with the cherries, onions, jalapeño, lime juice, and cilantro. Add the grains and combine. Garnish with the mint.

# Polenta and Orange Salad with Fennel Salsa (GF)

**Makes 4 servings**

¼ teaspoon sea salt

1 cup polenta

¼ cup Garlic-Ginger Oil (page 11)

1 tablespoon white wine vinegar

1 tablespoon chopped fresh cilantro, leaves and stems

1 tablespoon gluten-free tamari

1 tablespoon chopped peeled fresh ginger (from about a 1-inch piece)

1 teaspoon sugar

3 tablespoons olive oil

2 tablespoons orange juice, preferably freshly squeezed (from ½ medium orange)

4.5 ounces (6 cups) arugula, tough stems discarded

2 cups Fennel Salsa (recipe follows)

With its tamari and ginger, you might expect this robust dish to lean toward Asian flavors. Instead, the polenta and fennel lend it a more global taste, one that has depth and complexity but is also refreshingly bright. This is the sort of dish I think of when I talk about Northwest cuisine. The salsa was inspired by a *Bon Appétit* version paired with fish; I prefer polenta.

---

Bring 3 cups of water and the salt to a boil in a large saucepan. Add the polenta and cook, stirring frequently, until it thickens, about 10 minutes. Stir in the garlic-ginger oil, being sure to include a generous amount of the ginger and garlic pieces.

Spread the polenta in an 8- or 9-inch square baking pan. Cover and refrigerate for at least 4 to 5 hours or overnight.

When you're ready to prepare the salad, cut the polenta into 8 discs with a cookie cutter or glass dipped in flour. (For an extra layer of flavor before reheating, spray the cakes with cooking spray, heat a grill to medium heat, and cook the cakes for 1 to 2 minutes on each side, until distinct grill marks form.) To reheat the cakes, heat a stovetop grill pan on medium. Add the cakes, along with 1 to 2 tablespoons of water, just enough to steam them. Cook them for 3 minutes on each side, or until warmed through.

In a medium bowl, make an orange-cilantro vinaigrette by whisking together the vinegar, cilantro, tamari, ginger, sugar, olive oil, and orange juice. In a large bowl, combine the arugula and fennel salsa. Dress the mixture with ¼ cup of the vinaigrette.

Divide the salad among 4 plates and arrange 2 polenta cakes alongside the greens on each.

# Fennel Salsa

In a medium bowl, combine the oil, vinegar, cilantro, tamari, ginger, and sugar. Gently stir in the oranges, fennel, and onion. Season to taste with salt and pepper.

Any leftover salsa will keep a good 2 weeks in the refrigerator. It makes a great salad dressing, or you could use it as a condiment on a sandwich or in a wrap.

**Makes 5 cups**

2 tablespoons olive oil

2 tablespoons white wine vinegar

2 tablespoons chopped fresh cilantro, leaves and stems

2 teaspoons gluten-free tamari

2 teaspoons minced peeled fresh ginger

2 teaspoons sugar

3 medium oranges, peeled, segmented, and pith and membranes removed

1 medium fennel bulb, trimmed and sliced into ¼-inch-wide by 2-inch-long matchsticks (about 1½ cups)

½ cup thinly sliced red onion

Sea salt and freshly ground pepper

# Apple Ginger Salad (SF/GF)

This crunchy salad can be a catchall for almost any vegetable and fruit you have on hand. In the springtime, I might use snap peas instead of beans. In the summer, strawberries can take the place of the apples, or substitute carrots—they're crunchy and carry a hint of sweetness too. The tart dressing is a match for almost any ingredients.

---

Fill a large cooking pot with 4 quarts of water and the salt. Bring the water to a boil, add the beans, and cook for about 1 minute, until the colors brighten but the beans still have a crunch. Drain the beans and run cold water over them to stop them from cooking further. Refrigerate the beans for 10 minutes.

In a large bowl, combine the cooked beans with the apple, bell pepper, tomato, onion, and greens.

In a small bowl, whisk the garlic-ginger oil and lime juice. Season to taste with salt and pepper and toss with the salad.

**Makes 4 servings**

1 teaspoon sea salt

8 ounces green or yellow beans, ends trimmed

1 medium green apple, cut into ½-inch wedges

1 medium red or yellow bell pepper, cut into ¼-inch matchsticks (about 1 cup)

1 medium tomato, cut into ½-inch wedges

½ small red onion, thinly sliced

4 cups greens, preferably spring mix

½ cup Garlic-Ginger Oil (page 11)

Juice of 1 medium lime

Sea salt and freshly ground pepper

# Avocado Salad with Seitan Bites

**Makes 6 servings**

1 tablespoon olive oil

8 ounces seitan, cut into ½-inch cubes

½ cup canola oil, divided

1 heaping teaspoon cumin

1 medium bunch cilantro, stemmed and leaves chopped (about 1 cup)

1 teaspoon garlic powder

1 heaping teaspoon sea salt

1 medium jalapeño, seeded and chopped

½ teaspoon crushed red pepper flakes

3 tablespoons freshly squeezed lime juice (from 2 medium limes)

3 medium avocados, peeled, pitted, and cut into ½-inch cubes

2 medium tomatoes, cut into ½-inch cubes

1 large English cucumber, peeled and cut into ½-inch cubes

½ small red onion, cut into thin half-moons

Ripe, creamy avocados are irresistible in season and lend themselves to so much more than the usual guacamoles and salsas. This fun, substantial midsummer salad is a good way to use up your extra avocados, with the seitan adding some meaty weight to the dish and the cukes contributing some crunch. Sautéing the cumin first makes it smooth and smoky.

---

Heat the olive oil in a small sauté pan over medium heat. Cook the seitan, flipping the pieces with a spatula until all sides are browned, about 3 to 5 minutes. Remove the pan from the heat and let the seitan cool while you make the salad.

Heat ¼ cup of the canola oil in a small saucepan over medium heat. Add the cumin and cook until the cumin is golden brown, about 1 minute. In a medium bowl, mix the cumin and its oil, the remaining ¼ cup canola oil, cilantro, garlic powder, salt, jalapeño, red pepper flakes, and lime juice. Whisk until well combined, or blend in a blender or the bowl of a food processor for a sharper flavor.

In a large serving bowl, gently combine the avocados, tomatoes, cucumber, and onion. Add the seitan, and pour the dressing over all.

# Blood Orange and Fresh Tofu Salad (GF)

This fresh salad is full of standard Mediterranean flavors, but I like the interesting, healthier slant it acquires by using firm tofu as a centerpiece rather than feta or goat cheese. Blood oranges are visually striking, but if they're out of season, any orange will do.

_____

In a large bowl, season the tofu cubes with salt and pepper to taste. Add the orange, cilantro, onion, mint, oil, lemon juice, and coriander, and toss well. Serve immediately.

**Makes 4 servings**

8 ounces firm tofu, cut into ½-inch cubes

Sea salt and freshly ground pepper

1 medium blood orange, peeled and sliced into ¼-inch-thick half-moons

½ cup loosely packed fresh cilantro leaves

¼ cup thinly sliced red onion

¼ cup mint leaves

2 tablespoons olive oil

1 tablespoon freshly squeezed lemon juice

1 teaspoon coriander

# Roasted Beet and Blood Orange Salad with Cilantro Pesto (SF/GF)

**Makes 4 servings**

1 pound (about 3 to 5 medium) red or golden beets

¼ cup extra-virgin olive oil

1 tablespoon chopped garlic

1 medium blood orange, peeled and cut into ¼-inch rounds

½ cup Cilantro Pesto (recipe follows)

Sea salt and coarsely ground pepper or crushed peppercorns

2 tablespoons chopped fresh cilantro, for garnish

Beets tend to be underused and underappreciated—until people taste them at their fresh best, rather than the canned pickled version. The lovely deep maroon or golden colors of fresh beets shine here against the crimson blood oranges, and the citrus brightens up the rough, earthy flavor of the beets. Use a regular orange if blood oranges aren't in season. You can make the pesto up to a day ahead.

Preheat the oven to 350 degrees F.

Rub the beets all over with the oil and garlic, and put them in a covered roasting pan or casserole dish. (Or, after rubbing, tightly wrap each beet in aluminum foil.) Roast them for about 45 minutes, until fork-tender.

Remove the pan from the oven and let the beets cool.

When the beets are cool enough to handle, cut them into ¼-inch rounds. Put them in a large serving bowl with the oranges and gently toss with the pesto. Season to taste with salt and pepper.

To serve, arrange the beet and orange rounds on 4 plates in an overlapping pattern, and garnish each with a pinch of cilantro and salt and pepper to taste.

# Cilantro Pesto (SF/GF)

To toast the pine nuts, heat a small dry skillet over medium-low heat. Put in the pine nuts and toast for a few minutes, tossing or stirring frequently, until the nuts are fragrant and lightly browned. Let the pine nuts cool before using.

Put the pine nuts, oil, cilantro, chives, mint, jalapeño, garlic, salt, and pepper in a blender or the bowl of a food processor. Puree until smooth. Cover and chill.

Just before you're ready to use the pesto, reblend it if it has separated and whisk in the lime juice.

**Makes about 1 cup**

¼ cup pine nuts

½ cup extra-virgin olive oil

½ large bunch cilantro, coarsely chopped (about 2 cups)

½ medium bunch chives, coarsely chopped (about 1 tablespoon)

¼ cup packed fresh mint leaves

1 tablespoon chopped jalapeño

1 small garlic clove, peeled

1 scant teaspoon coarse sea salt

½ teaspoon freshly ground pepper

3 tablespoons freshly squeezed lime juice (from 2 medium limes)

# Grilled Peach and Arugula Salad with Soy Ricotta and Grilled Sourdough Toast

**Makes 4 servings**

1 tablespoon canola oil

1½ cups Basil Soy Ricotta (page 8)

2 medium peaches, halved, pitted, and cut into ½-inch wedges

Sea salt and freshly ground pepper

Vegetable oil cooking spray

8 thick slices sourdough bread, divided

6 ounces (8 cups) arugula, tough stems discarded

Agave Balsamic Vinaigrette (page 9)

Peaches have a short season in the Northwest, and their fleeting presence makes them all the more precious. I look forward all year to grilling ripe peaches and pairing those gorgeous, sweet, orange slices with bitter greens.

---

Heat the oil in a medium skillet over medium-high heat. Add the ricotta and cook for 5 to 10 minutes, stirring occasionally, until it browns on the bottom and acquires a drier texture. Set aside.

Slice peach halves into 16 wedges and season with salt and pepper to taste.

Heat a stovetop grill pan over high heat. Spray both the grill and the peaches with the cooking spray. Grill the peaches for about 30 seconds on each side, or until distinct grill marks form. (Be sure to only briefly sear them; they shouldn't be on the grill long enough to soften.) Remove the peaches to a large bowl and let them briefly cool.

Spray 4 slices of the bread with cooking spray and grill for 30 seconds or so on each side, until it is lightly toasted and has distinct grill marks.

Add the arugula to the bowl with the peaches, gently toss, and dress with the balsamic vinaigrette to taste. Divide the dressed greens and peaches among 4 plates, crumbling the ricotta evenly over all. Serve with the remaining slices of sourdough on the side.

# Creamy Millet Corn Chowder (SF/GF)

This is a more substantial version of a standard corn chowder, adapted from a recipe from Deborah Madison, whose cookbooks helped lead the way toward seeing vegetarian food as gourmet. I use millet here, which is rich in fiber and minerals. Feel free to substitute frozen corn if fresh isn't in season—corn is one of the few vegetables whose sweet taste from the field fades so fast you're better off using good-quality frozen kernels than old, starchy cobs.

---

In a medium stockpot, bring 7 cups of water to a boil. Add the millet and cook until it's barely tender, about 15 minutes. Drain the millet, reserving the cooking liquid.

In a medium stockpot, heat the oil over medium heat. Add the garlic and jalapeño and sauté until the garlic begins to lightly brown, about 30 seconds. Add the cumin, potatoes, and 6 cups of the reserved millet cooking liquid, and bring to a boil.

Add the cooked millet and reduce the heat to a simmer. Cook until the potatoes are tender, about 15 minutes. Stir in the corn and green onions (if you're using frozen corn, let it cook for a few minutes, until it is soft). Add the spinach, and season to taste with salt and pepper. Garnish the soup with the cilantro.

**Makes 4 servings**

¾ cup millet, rinsed well

2 tablespoons olive oil

1 garlic clove, finely chopped

1 small jalapeño, seeded and finely diced

½ teaspoon ground cumin

2 baby purple or red potatoes, diced

1 cup fresh or frozen corn kernels

3 green onions, thinly sliced, both white and tender green parts

4 ounces (about 2 cups) baby spinach leaves

Sea salt and freshly ground pepper

⅓ cup chopped fresh cilantro, leaves and stems, for garnish

# Habanero Yam Soup (SF/GF)

I love spicy foods, and habaneros are among the hottest peppers you can find. If your own tolerance for spice is lower, you can cut the amount back to only half a pepper. Either way, wear plastic gloves when seeding and chopping the pepper, being careful not to touch your eyes. This dish is best in fall and winter, when yams are at the height of their season and have the most well-developed flavors.

Preheat the oven to 400 degrees F.

Rub the yams all over with 1 tablespoon of the oil and roast them in a large baking pan until they are fork-tender, 30 to 45 minutes. Remove the pan from the oven and let them cool slightly.

Heat the remaining 3 tablespoons of oil in a small stockpot over medium heat. Add the green onions, garlic, and habanero and sauté until they are soft, 1 to 2 minutes. Add the roasted yams, scooping the flesh from inside the peels if you baked them in their skins, and mix. Add 2 cups of the stock.

In a blender or the bowl of a food processor, puree the soup in batches, adding another 1 to 2 cups of stock, depending how thick you want the soup, and taking care with the hot liquid. (Or, puree the soup in the stockpot with an immersion blender.) Return the soup to the stockpot and bring it to a boil. Season to taste with salt and pepper.

**Makes 4 servings**

3¼ pounds (about 4 medium) red-skinned yams (peeling optional)

4 tablespoons olive oil, divided

1 medium bunch green onions, both white and green parts, chopped (about 1 cup)

1 tablespoon finely chopped garlic

1 habanero pepper, seeded and chopped

1 quart gluten-free vegetable stock (such as Imagine brand or homemade), divided

Sea salt and freshly ground pepper

# Cauliflower Bisque with Fresh Fennel (GF)

**Makes 4 servings**

⅓ cup olive oil, divided

¼ cup minced smoked tofu (such as Baba's Mesquite Tofu)

1 tablespoon chopped garlic

1 leek (white and pale green parts only), rinsed well and thinly sliced

¾ medium fennel bulb, trimmed and cut into ¼-inch matchsticks, 1 tablespoon chopped fronds reserved

1 cup water

2 cups unsweetened soy milk

1 pound (about 3½ cups) cauliflower florets

¼ cup chopped fresh parsley, plus 2 tablespoons for garnish

2 tablespoons freshly squeezed lemon juice (from 1 medium lemon)

1 cup Savory Soy Cream (page 6), plus ¼ cup for garnish

Sea salt and freshly ground pepper

Cauliflower doesn't often get the glamour gigs, but it's good for way more than a crudités plate. Here I feature it in a silky, creamy soup, helped along by licorice-flavored fennel.

In a small sauté pan, heat 2 tablespoons of the oil over medium heat. Add the minced tofu and sauté 2 to 3 minutes, until crisp and golden-brown.

Heat the remaining oil in a medium stockpot over medium heat. Add the garlic, leek, and ⅔ of the fennel matchsticks (reserving the rest for garnish), and sauté until lightly browned, about 8 minutes. Add the water, milk, cauliflower, and ¼ cup of the parsley. Cook until the cauliflower is soft to the point of mushiness, about 15 minutes. Add the lemon juice (or more to taste)—it will curdle the soy milk, but don't panic; it's supposed to do that.

Puree the soup in batches in a blender or the bowl of a food processor with 1 cup of the soy cream (or add the soy cream to the pot and blend with an immersion blender), taking care with the hot liquid. When the soup is creamy and smooth, season to taste with salt and pepper.

To serve, divide the soup among 4 bowls, spooning 1 tablespoon of the soy cream garnish in the center of each. Arrange a quarter of the remaining fennel matchsticks on top of the cream in each bowl. Add 1½ teaspoons of the browned minced tofu in its oil to each, and sprinkle each with ½ tablespoon of the parsley garnish and ¼ tablespoon of the reserved fennel fronds.

# Raw Kale and Seaweed Salad with Fresh Tofu and Ginger-Garlic Oil (GF)

Cool-weather kale is so abundant in the Northwest, I wanted to find some way to appreciate it beyond raw green smoothies or spicy braised greens. When I was on a raw fast, I discovered that kale shines in a raw salad: the leaves are hardy, but they're sweet and amazingly mild. Use dried seaweed here for crunch, or reconstitute the seaweed and serve the salad with steamed rice.

---

In a small bowl, combine the oil, tamari (or more to taste), lime juice, and red pepper flakes, and season to taste with salt and pepper.

In a large bowl, mix the kale, cabbage, tofu, and seaweed. Gently toss the salad with the dressing and serve.

**Makes 4 servings**

½ cup Garlic-Ginger Oil (page 11)

1 tablespoon gluten-free tamari

2 tablespoons freshly squeezed lime juice (from 1 medium lime)

Pinch of crushed red pepper flakes

Sea salt and freshly ground pepper

2 medium bunches kale, stemmed and chopped into ½-inch pieces (about 8 cups)

¼ small head red cabbage, shredded (about 1 cup)

8 ounces regular or firm tofu, cut into ½-inch cubes

2 tablespoons seaweed (such as Eden brand wakame), dried or reconstituted in ½ cup hot water for a chewy texture

# Small Plates

At the restaurant, small plates are a great draw for omnivores, and I like to provide dishes that attract meat-eaters as well as people who already know they like vegan food. Make these small plates separately as appetizers, or put together an assortment for a varied, dinner party–style meal. All of them are small bites with really big flavors, and it's fun to have a group of friends over to try a bunch of different dishes. For my own party, I'd serve Curried Red Yam Fries (page 56), Jerk Tofu and Roasted Yam Sliders (page 61), and Spicy Chili-Lime Edamame (page 55).

# Charred Broccolini (SF/GF)

Broccolini, a sweet, stalky hybrid of broccoli and *gai lan*, Chinese kale (also known as Chinese broccoli), gets a smoky, spicy treatment here, set off with a bright punch of lemon. Try it and you'll never look twice at bland brassicas again. A gas stove or gas grill really is best here to get the smoky flavor and char. If you have trouble finding broccolini, cauliflower tastes great cooked the same way.

---

In a large frying pan, heat the oil over high heat. Add the garlic, which will immediately start to brown, then add the bell pepper. Cook for 1 minute, stirring with a wooden spoon or spatula, until the pepper starts to sizzle, then add the broccolini. Shake the pan a bit so the gas flame leaps inside (be careful, of course!) and begins to blacken the broccolini in spots. Flip the broccolini with a pair of tongs if the shaking hasn't turned them already, and cook for a moment until the other side begins to char at the edges. After another minute or so, when the blackened broccolini starts to wilt, squeeze the lemon halves over the vegetables. (You don't want to squish the lemons dry; just squeeze out a good sprinkle of juice.) The broccolini will start to smoke, adding to the flavor. Sprinkle the vegetables with the red pepper flakes, adding more to taste, and season with salt and pepper to taste. Give the pan another gentle toss and remove it from the heat.

**Makes 4 servings**

¼ cup olive oil

2 teaspoons chopped garlic

½ medium red bell pepper, cut into ¼-inch matchsticks (about ½ cup)

12 ounces broccolini, trimmed, stalks separated but left intact

1 medium lemon, halved

½ teaspoon crushed red pepper flakes

Sea salt and freshly ground pepper

# Smashed Purple Potatoes with Parsley (SF/GF)

**Makes 4 servings**

1 pound (about 8) baby purple potatoes

¼ cup plus 3 tablespoons olive oil, divided

3 garlic cloves, minced

Sea salt and freshly ground pepper

2 tablespoons chopped fresh parsley

1 tablespoon chopped fresh rosemary leaves

Zest and juice of 1 medium lemon

These potatoes are doubly addictive, with the appeal of mashed potatoes and crisp fried potatoes combined in one dish. The bonus is how pretty they are too, a natural violet color that they retain even after they're cooked. Purple potatoes sound exotic, but many large supermarkets carry them now. You can substitute thyme, chives, or other favorite herbs for the rosemary, or use less rosemary for a more subtle flavor.

---

Preheat the over to 450 degrees F.

Bring a large pot of salted water to a boil. Add the potatoes and cook until they are fork-tender, about 8 minutes. Drain and set aside.

Drizzle ¼ cup of the oil all over a large sheet pan or cookie sheet. Place the boiled potatoes on the sheet, leaving plenty of room between each one.

With a potato masher or the flat end of a spatula—or even your hands if the potatoes are cool enough—gently press down on each potato until the top gives way and the insides are lightly crushed. Rotate the pan 90 degrees and mash the potatoes again more forcefully, until they are slightly flattened. The idea is to open up the potato enough to let in the flavors of the garlic and herbs. Brush the tops of each crushed potato generously with the remaining 3 tablespoons of oil.

Sprinkle the potatoes with the garlic and season to taste with salt and pepper. Bake until they are browned, 20 to 25 minutes. Remove them from the oven and sprinkle the parsley, rosemary, and lemon zest and juice over the top before serving.

# Chai-Spiced Yam Bruschetta with Crunchy Kale (SF)

**Makes 4 to 6 servings**

For the yams:

2¼ pounds (about 3 medium) red-skinned yams, peeled and halved lengthwise

2 tablespoons olive oil

1 tablespoon good-quality ground dry chai tea, or ¼ cup liquid chai concentrate

¼ cup canola oil

2 tablespoons chopped peeled fresh ginger (from about a 2-inch piece)

2 tablespoons chopped garlic

¼ cup (½ stick) soy-free vegan buttery spread (such as Earth Balance brand)

2 tablespoons light brown sugar

Sea salt and freshly ground pepper

For the kale:

1 to 2 tablespoons canola oil

½ teaspoon chopped garlic

1 small bunch kale, stemmed and leaves cut into thin ribbons

1 rustic baguette, cut diagonally into 1-inch-thick slices

1 tart apple, cored and cut into matchsticks, for garnish (optional)

2 tablespoons chopped pecans, for garnish (optional)

Everyone seems to love both sweet yams and aromatic chai. Marrying those flavors gives these yams a distinctly different twist than the usual cinnamon or nutmeg. I try to combine flavors people never would have thought of putting together, and this is one of the times when my experimentation came out just right. If you want a softer texture, use the chai concentrate instead of the tea.

---

Preheat the oven to 400 degrees F and line a baking sheet with aluminum foil or parchment paper for easy cleanup.

To make the yams, place them on the prepared baking sheet and drizzle them with the olive oil. If you're using ground chai, sprinkle it on the yams. Bake the yams until they're super soft, about 45 minutes. Transfer them to a large bowl.

In a small saucepan, heat the canola oil over medium heat. Sauté the ginger and garlic together for 3 to 5 minutes, until they're golden brown. Pour the mixture over the cooked yams and add the buttery spread, brown sugar, and chai concentrate, if using. Mash the yams with a potato masher or the back of a wooden spoon until they're smooth, and season to taste with salt and pepper. Set aside.

To make the kale, lightly coat the bottom of a large sauté pan with the oil. Heat the oil over medium heat, add the garlic, and cook until it's lightly browned, about 1 minute. Raise the heat to high and add the kale. Season to taste with salt and pepper and cook the kale for 1 to 2 minutes, tossing it occasionally with tongs or a spatula, until it is crisp and charred on the edges, but not burnt.

To assemble the bruschetta, spread a tablespoon or more of mashed yams on each baguette slice. Don't completely cover the slices; leave a border around the edges. Add a generous pinch of crunchy kale in the middle of each slice and garnish with a few pieces of apple and a sprinkle of pecans.

# Oven-Roasted Cherry Tomatoes with Thyme on Toast (SF)

Think of this simple dish as a fresher version of sun-dried tomatoes, concentrating all the bright flavors of summer at its best. We serve the tomatoes on toast, but you can also present them as a hot or cold side dish or add them to salads.

Preheat the oven to 250 degrees F and line a rimmed baking sheet with aluminum foil or parchment paper for easy cleanup.

In a small bowl, coat the tomatoes with the oil, garlic, and thyme. Spread the tomatoes on the prepared baking sheet and season to taste with salt and pepper. Bake for 1 to 2 hours, until the tomatoes wrinkle and collapse but still retain a bit of juice. Toast the bread and top each slice with a few spoonfuls of tomatoes, drizzling a little extra oil on top.

**Makes 4 servings**

1 pint heirloom cherry tomatoes, stems on

2 tablespoons olive oil, plus extra for drizzling the bread (optional)

1 tablespoon chopped garlic

1 teaspoon fresh thyme leaves

Sea salt and freshly ground pepper

4 thick slices sourdough bread

# Spicy Chili-Lime Edamame (GF)

Edamame (immature soybeans usually served in the pod) is tremen-dously popular these days, but it always seems to be served in the same plain way: boiled and sprinkled in salt. I wanted to do something a little more interesting that made it tastier on the outside as well as the inside. The result is bar food, snack food, dressed-up football-party food ... or just make a bowl for yourself and eat it all. It's that good.

Bring a large pot of water to a boil. Add the edamame and cook until tender, about 3 to 5 minutes (start counting when the water returns to a boil). Drain and transfer to a bowl to cool.

Heat the oil in a large sauté pan over medium-high heat. Add the garlic, ginger, and cooked edamame, and stir for about 2 minutes, until the gar-lic begins to brown and the pods are heated through. Add the lime juice and red pepper flakes and stir until the edamame are evenly coated. Transfer to a platter or bowl and serve immediately.

**Makes 4 servings**

1 pound unshelled fresh or frozen edamame

2 to 3 tablespoons canola oil

2 tablespoons chopped garlic

2 tablespoons chopped peeled fresh ginger (from about a 2-inch piece)

Juice of 1 medium lime

1 teaspoon crushed red pepper flakes

# Curried Red Yam Fries (SF/GF)

**Makes 4 servings**

1 quart canola oil

2 medium red-skinned yams, peels left on and cut into fries about 4 inches long by ¼ inch thick

1 tablespoon curry powder

2 teaspoons chopped fresh parsley, or 1 teaspoon chopped fresh dill or cilantro

Yam fries will never be quite as crisp as those made with russets, but the thinner you cut them, the crisper they'll be, and the yams' rich flavor more than makes up for the extra crunch. There's lots of leeway here to jazz up the spices. We sometimes use a Jamaican-style curry powder; you can doctor your basic curry powder with paprika or garlic or whatever you like. These fries are great either alone or with Lemon Dill Aioli (page 25) for dipping.

---

Heat the oil in a large, heavy-bottomed Dutch oven to 350 degrees F as measured on an instant-read thermometer.

Put the yams in a fry basket, lower it carefully into the hot oil, and cook until the fries rise to the top, 3 to 7 minutes depending on their thickness. (If you don't have a fry basket, gently lower the fries into the oil using a slotted spoon, being careful not to splatter the hot oil, then carefully remove them with a slotted spoon.)

Transfer the fries to a tray or bowl lined with paper towels. Toss them with the curry powder (adding more to taste) and parsley, and serve immediately.

# Grilled Wild Mushroom Toasts

**Makes 4 servings**

3 tablespoons vegan buttery spread (such as Earth Balance brand)

1 teaspoon chopped garlic

1 pound mixed wild mushrooms, cleaned and sliced

1 teaspoon chopped fresh thyme leaves, plus 3 tablespoons whole leaves

Sea salt and freshly ground pepper

¼ cup red wine vinegar

2 tablespoons vegan mayonnaise or Savory Soy Cream (page 6)

2 tablespoons chopped shallots

½ cup olive oil, plus more for brushing the toasts

I baguette, cut into slices ⅓ inch to ½ inch thick

½ cup Basil Soy Ricotta (page 8)

Foragers roam the Northwest for wild mushrooms, which are plentiful in the late summer and early fall. It's hard to go wrong with the taste of any sautéed mushrooms, so if wild ones aren't available, you can use regular white button mushrooms or oyster mushrooms. If you can, though, look in well-stocked markets or specialty stores for a mix that includes meaty little chanterelles or more unusual varieties such as black trumpets. Use the whole mushroom; discarding the stems would waste half the good flavor.

---

Melt the buttery spread in a large skillet over medium-high heat. Add the garlic and sauté until browned, about 1 to 2 minutes. Add the mushrooms and chopped thyme, and sauté until the mushrooms are browned, about 2 to 3 minutes. Season to taste with salt and pepper and set aside.

Put the whole thyme leaves, vinegar, mayonnaise, and shallots into a blender or the bowl of a food processor. Blend for about 10 seconds, until well combined. With the machine still running, gradually add the oil, blending until the mixture is smooth. Season to taste with salt and pepper and set aside.

Brush the baguette slices with the oil. Heat a stovetop grill. Toast the bread for 1 minute or so until grill marks form, and remove from the grill. (It's also OK to toast them in the oven or toaster oven.)

Spread about 2 teaspoons of the ricotta on each bread slice. Pile about 1 tablespoon of the sautéed mushrooms on each slice, and drizzle about 1 teaspoon of the thyme dressing over each.

# Charred Brussels Sprouts and Fingerling Potatoes with Crispy Smoked Tofu (GF)

Be sure to use canola oil to cook the brussels sprouts—it has a higher smoke point than alternatives such as olive oil, which would burn on the high heat used to char the sprouts.

Preheat the oven to 400 degrees F and line a baking sheet with aluminum foil or parchment paper for easy cleanup.

Fill a large bowl with ice and water and set it in the sink.

Bring a large pot of salted water to a boil and cook the sprouts for 3 to 4 minutes, until they turn bright green but are not cooked through. Drain and transfer to the ice bath.

In a large bowl, toss the potatoes with the olive oil and 1 tablespoon of the garlic. Season to taste with salt and pepper. Spread the potatoes on the prepared baking sheet and bake until they are fork-tender, 15 to 20 minutes.

While the potatoes are baking, heat a cast-iron skillet over high heat. Add 1 tablespoon of the canola oil and about ⅓ of the brussels sprouts. Cook until the sprouts start to turn golden-brown, then add ⅓ of the remaining 1 tablespoon garlic and about ⅓ of the tofu. Toss and continue cooking until the sprouts start to char and blacken, about 1 minute. (They'll give off smoke in the process.) Transfer the mixture to a bowl and repeat with the rest of the canola oil, brussels sprouts, garlic, and tofu, cooking them in 2 more batches. When all are cooked, add a squeeze of juice from the lemon and season to taste with salt and pepper. Slice the lemon, mix the sprout mixture with the baked fingerlings either in the bowl or on a platter, and serve with the lemon slices.

**Makes 4 servings**

1 pound brussels sprouts, trimmed and halved

1 pound fingerling potatoes

2 tablespoons olive oil

2 tablespoons chopped garlic, divided

Sea salt and freshly ground pepper

3 tablespoons canola oil, divided

4 ounces smoked tofu (such as Baba's Mesquite Tofu), minced and divided

1 small lemon

# Jerk Tofu and Roasted Yam Sliders

Jamaican-spiced tofu makes for great little party burgers. We cut the spice with pickled cabbage for a huge punch of flavor. We make our own Jamaican tofu, Baba's Jerk Tofu, but if you can't get ours, you can substitute any national brand of spicy tofu. Note that you'll need to start the pickled cabbage at least 12 hours in advance, but it will keep, refrigerated, for a few weeks.

**Makes 4 servings**

1 small red-skinned yam, unpeeled and cut into ½-inch-thick slices

2 tablespoons olive oil, divided

1 to 2 packages Baba's Jerk Tofu, sliced ⅛ inch thick

¼ cup vegan mayonnaise or Savory Soy Cream (page 6)

1½ tablespoons yellow mustard

1 tablespoon sweet relish

8 mini burger buns, split

1 cup Pickled Purple Cabbage (recipe follows)

2 tablespoons chopped fresh Italian parsley

---

Preheat the oven to 400 degrees F.

Coat the yam slices lightly in about ½ tablespoon of the oil and put them in a small roasting pan. Cook them until they're quite tender, about 30 minutes. Set aside to cool.

In a large sauté pan, heat the remaining 1½ tablespoons of oil over medium heat. Sauté the tofu slices for 1 to 2 minutes on each side, until they're warmed through.

In a small bowl, whisk together the mayonnaise, mustard, and relish. Spread a dab on the top of each bun, then add a slice of yam to the bottom. Top with a slice of sautéed tofu and 1 or 2 tablespoons of cabbage, depending on how much kick you prefer. Sprinkle some parsley over each, add the top buns, and serve.

## Pickled Purple Cabbage (SF/GF)

**Makes about 2 cups**

1 medium red onion, thinly sliced

½ cup malt vinegar

¼ cup canola oil

Juice of 1 small lime or lemon

1 tablespoon evaporated cane juice (sugar) or agave syrup

1 tablespoon chopped fresh basil

1 small jalapeño, seeded and chopped

1 teaspoon sea salt

1 teaspoon freshly ground pepper

½ head small purple cabbage, shredded (4 to 5 cups)

In a large bowl, combine the onion, vinegar, oil, lime juice, cane juice, basil, jalapeño, salt, and pepper. Stir until the cane juice is completely dissolved. Add the cabbage and stir until it's well coated. Cover and let stand at room temperature for 12 to 24 hours, depending how strong you want the taste, mixing it once or twice. Refrigerate until ready to use.

To make a batch of pickled red onions, simply omit the cabbage.

# Barbecue Oyster Mushroom Sliders with Pickled Onions

**Makes 4 servings**

¼ cup olive oil

1 teaspoon chopped garlic

1 pound oyster mushrooms, cleaned and pulled apart into 1-inch pieces

¾ cup plus 2 tablespoons vegan barbecue sauce, divided

¼ cup vegan mayonnaise or Savory Soy Cream (page 6)

8 mini burger buns, split

½ cup pickled red onions (see Pickled Purple Cabbage recipe, page 61)

1 tablespoon chopped fresh parsley

These sliders are savory, hearty, dinner-party bites. Use your favorite smoky barbecue sauce and spark up the sliders further with our spicy, tangy pickled onions. You won't miss the meat. To make the dish soy-free, substitute a rice milk mayonnaise.

Heat the oil in a large pan over medium-high heat. Add the garlic and cook until browned, 1 to 2 minutes. Add the mushrooms and toss them in the oil for a few minutes, until they are softened but retain their thick, meaty texture. Add ¾ cup of the barbecue sauce and lower the heat to a simmer, cooking the mixture for about 5 minutes, until the sauce has thickened and the flavor has penetrated the mushrooms. They should look like bits of pulled pork.

In a small bowl, whisk together the mayonnaise and the remaining 2 tablespoons of barbecue sauce to make a sort of aioli. Pile a few spoonfuls of mushrooms on the bottom of each bun. Add a drizzle of aioli and a tablespoon of pickled onions. Sprinkle chopped parsley over the onions, add the top buns, and serve.

# Manna Bread with Raw Tofu Relish and Cherry Salsa

We've heard of the biblical manna bread; the store-bought version is made from sprouted grains and baked at lower temperatures than conventional breads. It's cakey and slightly sweet. Look for it in the frozen foods section if you don't see it with the other breads. We serve ours in small slices piled with tofu and a sweet, juicy cherry relish adapted from author Romney Steele's book *Plum Gorgeous*. This is a good transitional dish for a raw-food diet (the manna and the toasted almonds in the salsa keep it from being a strictly raw-food meal).

**Makes 4 servings**

8 slices manna bread

1 cup Raw Tofu Relish (page 11)

1 cup Cherry Salsa (recipe follows)

8 fresh basil leaves, cut into ribbons, for garnish

Arrange 2 slices of manna bread on each of 4 plates. Pile 1 to 2 tablespoons of tofu relish on each, then top with 1 to 2 tablespoons of cherry salsa. Garnish each with 2 basil leaves.

## Cherry Salsa (SF/GF)

To toast the almonds, heat a small dry skillet over medium-low heat. Put in the almonds and toast for a few minutes, tossing or stirring frequently, until the nuts are fragrant and lightly browned. Let the almonds cool before using.

Combine the almonds, cherries, onion, jalapeño, lime juice, cilantro, mint, and agave syrup in a medium bowl. Season to taste with salt and pepper.

**Makes about 2 cups**

¼ cup almonds

8 ounces fresh cherries, pitted and halved (or quartered if large)

½ cup chopped red onion

1 small jalapeño, seeded and minced

2 tablespoons freshly squeezed lime juice (from 1 medium lime)

¼ cup chopped fresh cilantro, leaves and stems

A handful of mint leaves, cut into ribbons

1 tablespoon agave syrup

Sea salt and freshly ground pepper

# Tofu, Tempeh & Seitan

Cooking with substantial proteins such as tempeh, tofu, and seitan gives you the satisfaction of a hearty, protein-packed dinner—without the meat. These plant-based dishes will give your non-vegan guest an experience of a different kind of gratifying meal that will make them want to add the variety of veganism to their diet. In addition to your favorite local tofu brands, we make our own Makini's Kitchen brand of flavored tofus you can order online at PlumBistro. com. These robustly flavored tofus come in flavors such as Baba's Mesquite Tofu (a smoked tofu), Baba's Jerk Tofu (a Jamaican jerk–spiced tofu), Baba's Tofustrami (a pastrami-flavored tofu), and Baba's Taco Mix (perfect for tacos and beyond). They are sure to add excitement to your meals.

# What Are Tofu, Tempeh, And Seitan?

**TOFU**, a mild-flavored bean curd made from coagulated soy milk, is probably the best-known vegan protein. I always like to tell people, "Don't be afraid of the tofu!" People see it as this white, spongy, incomprehensible substance, but it's easy to use and useful. Tofu absorbs flavors well when it's marinated long enough, and it lends itself to frying. It comes in different textures, from soft to extra firm. The softer varieties make for a good breakfast scramble; they give you more of an egglike feeling, but also break up easily. I prefer silken tofu, which has the mildest flavor and an eggy feel. Use firm tofu for steaklike dishes and entrées. Extra-firm will give you the most substantial texture, but remember that it will absorb flavors differently, and your sauces won't penetrate it as easily as they will the softer varieties.

I probably get asked, "What is **TEMPEH**?" ten times a day in the restaurant. People know tofu but aren't as familiar with this cultured product, made from whole soybeans that are cooked and cured in a gourmet cheese-like process. For me, tempeh is the hipper, cooler little sister of the vegan diet. It's less processed than tofu, has no cholesterol, and is packed with nutritious vitamins, minerals, and essential fatty acids. It's also probably my favorite protein to work with, because cakes of tempeh are more versatile than tofu or seitan. Tempeh sautés well; it marinates really well; and its texture and earthy flavor make it a delicious substitute for fish. To me, it holds flavors a little better than raw tofu does, with a more interesting and sophisticated taste and texture. There are plain tempehs as well as multigrain versions. We use both; choose whichever one you prefer, but use plain tempeh for gluten-free dishes.

**SEITAN** is a chewy wheat gluten derived from flour, with a texture that's much closer to meat than other vegan products. The taste is not at all meaty—there's no blood in it, after all—but the texture is interchangeable with beef or chicken. I use it when I want a really hearty dish, but I don't rely excessively on it because people with gluten sensitivities and celiac disease can't eat it.

# Spicy Peach Tofu and Tempeh with Charred Purple Beans

I love this spicy, bright, smoky-sweet dish, alive with the flavors of lime and chipotle. Use a sweet riesling when making it. It's a great use for peaches that have gone over the edge of ripeness—you want the fruit to be so soft that it'll smush easily into juicy pieces for your marinade. If you don't have a gas range for the charred beans or you want to keep more of their intense purple color intact, you can toss them with olive oil, salt, and pepper, and grill them for a minute or two instead.

---

In a large bowl, smash the peaches until the flesh comes off the pit in chunks. Discard the pits. Add the wine, cilantro, sugar, lime juice, 1 cup of the oil, chipotles, roasted garlic, salt, and pepper and mix well. Spread a thin layer of this marinade in a shallow, medium baking pan, reserving the rest.

Heat a stovetop or outdoor grill to high heat.

Spray the tempeh and tofu slices evenly with cooking spray on both sides. Grill them for about 1 to 2 minutes on each side, flipping them with a long spatula, until distinct hash marks form. Transfer them to the baking pan, setting them atop the marinade and pouring the reserved marinade over. Cover the pan and refrigerate for 5 to 6 hours, or up to overnight for more flavor.

In a large skillet, heat the remaining ¼ cup oil over high heat. Add the chopped garlic and cook for a few seconds. Add the beans, cooking them in 2 batches if the pan is crowded. If you're cooking on a gas stove, shake the pan a bit so the flame leaps inside and begins to blacken the beans in spots. Shake or use tongs to turn the beans, and cook them for another minute, until the other side begins to char at the edges and the garlic begins to brown. Remove them from the heat and season to taste with salt and pepper.

Heat a medium sauté pan or stovetop griddle over medium heat. Remove the tofu and tempeh slices from the marinade with a slotted spatula. (The marinade can be reserved for a second use or used in the

**Makes 4 servings**

2 unpeeled very ripe peaches

2 cups white wine, preferably riesling

1 cup (about 2 ounces) chopped fresh cilantro leaves

2 tablespoons sugar

½ cup freshly squeezed lime juice (from about 4 medium limes)

1¼ cups olive oil, divided

1 (7-ounce) can chipotle peppers in adobo sauce, minced (¾ cup)

⅔ cup Roasted Garlic Cloves (page 10), with a few cloves smashed

2 teaspoons sea salt

2 teaspoons freshly ground pepper

1 (8-ounce) pack soy or multigrain tempeh, cut crosswise into four ¼-inch-thick pieces

1 pound firm or extra-firm tofu (preferably your favorite local brand), cut lengthwise into five ½-inch-thick pieces

Olive oil cooking spray

1 teaspoon chopped garlic

1 pound purple or green beans, trimmed

1 cup Spicy Peach Sauce (recipe follows)

*continued*

spicy peach sauce.) Working in batches, cook the slices until they're browned and heated through, 3 to 4 minutes on each side.

To serve, put ¼ of the beans in each of 4 shallow bowls, arrange a slice of tofu and tempeh on top, and spoon ¼ cup peach sauce over everything.

## Spicy Peach Sauce

**Makes about 1 ¼ cups**

1 tablespoon olive oil

½ medium peach, chopped

1 tablespoon chopped canned chipotle peppers in adobo sauce

8 Roasted Garlic Cloves (page 10), or pick out the cloves from the tofu marinade

1 cup white wine

1 to 2 pinches sugar

¼ cup freshly squeezed lime juice (from about 2 medium limes)

Sea salt and freshly ground pepper

2 teaspoons chopped fresh cilantro

1½ tablespoons vegan buttery spread (such as Earth Balance brand)

Heat the oil in a large sauté pan over medium-high heat. Add the peach, chipotles (or more to taste), and garlic, and cook for 1 to 2 minutes, or until the mixture starts to brown. Carefully pour in the wine—it will bubble vigorously or even flame up on a gas range. Reduce the heat to a simmer, and add the sugar and lime juice. Season with salt and pepper to taste. Let the sauce simmer for 4 to 5 minutes, until it has slightly reduced. Remove from the heat. Add the cilantro and buttery spread and stir until the spread has melted and is thoroughly incorporated into the sauce.

# Balsamic Tofu with White Bean Sauce and Agave Pumpkins (GF)

Searing the tofu before it's marinated seals it in a way that allows it to absorb flavor evenly from the marinade. It also gives you attractive grill marks without risking burning the sweet sauce. When choosing pumpkins, the small edible heirloom varieties add great shades of color and flavor.

To make the tofu, in a large bowl make a marinade by combining the vinegar, onion, thyme, marjoram, cane juice, oil, lemon juice, parsley, garlic, salt, and pepper. Pour ¼ cup of the marinade into a shallow, medium baking pan, reserving the rest.

Heat a stovetop or outdoor grill to high heat.

Spray the tofu pieces evenly with cooking spray on both sides. Grill for about 1 to 2 minutes on each side, flipping them with a long spatula, until distinct hash marks form. Transfer to the baking pan, setting them atop the marinade and pouring the reserved marinade over. Cover the pan and refrigerate for 2 to 3 hours (or up to 8 hours for more flavor, but no longer, because the tofu will become very tart).

Preheat the oven to 400 degrees F and line a baking sheet with aluminum foil or parchment paper for easy cleanup.

To make the pumpkins, halve them, remove the stems, and, using a spoon, scrape out the seeds and discard (or save them to clean and roast later). Slice them into 1- to 2-inch crescents. In a large bowl, combine the agave syrup, 1 tablespoon of the oil, salt, and pepper. Coat the pumpkins with the mixture. Place the pumpkins on the prepared baking sheet and roast until they are fork-tender, 15 to 20 minutes. Let them cool, then toss them with the arugula and remaining 2 tablespoons oil. Set aside.

To make the sauce, heat the oil in a small sauté pan over medium heat. Add the sun-dried tomatoes, garlic, onion, and beans, and sauté for a few minutes until the garlic is golden brown. Reduce the heat to medium-low and stir in the reserved bean liquid, vinegar, parsley, cane juice, salt, and pepper. Turn off the heat. Quickly stir in the buttery spread until it melts and incorporates into the sauce and the sauce turns opaque.

*continued*

## Makes 4 servings

For the balsamic tofu:

1 cup balsamic vinegar, preferably a good-quality aged variety

½ cup finely chopped red onion

2 teaspoons chopped fresh thyme

2 teaspoons chopped fresh marjoram

2 teaspoons evaporated cane juice

1 cup canola or vegetable oil

¼ cup lemon juice (from 2 medium lemons)

⅓ cup chopped fresh parsley

1 tablespoon minced garlic

2 teaspoons sea salt

2 teaspoons freshly ground pepper

1 to 2 pounds firm or extra-firm tofu (preferably your favorite local brand), cut lengthwise into five ½-inch-thick pieces

Vegetable oil cooking spray

For the agave pumpkins:

4 baby pumpkins, any variety with sweet flesh and edible skin (such as Baby Bear)

1 tablespoon agave syrup

3 tablespoons olive oil, divided

Sea salt and freshly ground pepper

2 ounces (2 cups) arugula, tough stems discarded

For the white bean sauce:

½ cup olive oil

4 sun-dried tomatoes (or use leftover Oven-Roasted Cherry Tomatoes, page 53)

1 teaspoon chopped garlic

2 tablespoons finely diced red onion

¼ cup plus 2 tablespoons canned white beans, reserving ¼ cup bean liquid

¼ cup balsamic vinegar

¼ cup chopped fresh parsley

2 teaspoons evaporated cane juice

¼ teaspoon sea salt

¼ teaspoon freshly ground pepper

¼ cup (½ stick) vegan buttery spread (such as Earth Balance brand)

Heat a medium sauté pan or stovetop griddle over medium heat. Remove the tofu pieces from the marinade with a slotted spatula and, working in batches, cook them until they're heated through and crispy on the outside, 1 to 2 minutes on each side.

To serve, divide the pumpkin salad among 4 plates. Top each with 2 pieces of tofu, and drizzle the white bean sauce on top.

# Pesto Tofu with Smashed Purple Potatoes and Charred Asparagus (GF)

Sometimes it's hard to get tofu to absorb a tasty marinade. In this recipe I use a spicier sauce to impart flavor, but the dish doesn't end up super spicy, just nice and flavorful. It's one of Plum's most popular.

---

To make the tofu, put the garlic, onion, and olives in the bowl of a food processor and pulse until finely chopped (it's important to stop before the mixture turns to a smooth puree). Add the parsley and oregano and pulse briefly, 1 to 2 seconds, until the herbs are also finely chopped but not pureed. Or, if working by hand, finely mince the ingredients with a sharp knife and combine in a small mixing bowl. Transfer the mixture to a medium bowl. Add the oil, lime juice, vinegar, paprika, sugar, cayenne, and red pepper flakes (or more to taste), and stir until the sugar dissolves. Season to taste with salt. Pour ¼ cup of this marinade into a shallow, medium baking pan, reserving the rest.

Heat a stovetop or outdoor grill to high heat.

Spray the tofu pieces evenly with cooking spray on both sides. Grill them for about 1 to 2 minutes on each side, flipping them with a long spatula, until distinct hash marks form. Transfer them to the baking pan, setting them atop the marinade and pouring the reserved marinade over. Cover the pan and refrigerate for 8 to 12 hours (or up to overnight for more flavor).

To make the potatoes, preheat the oven to 450 degrees F, and line large sheet pan or cookie sheet with aluminum foil or parchment paper for easy cleanup.

Bring a large pot of salted water to a boil. Add the potatoes and boil them until they're fork-tender, about 10 minutes. Drain the potatoes.

Drizzle ¼ cup of the oil all over the prepared pan. Place the boiled potatoes on the sheet, leaving plenty of room between each one. With a potato masher or the flat end of a spatula—or even your hands if the potatoes are cool enough—gently press down on each potato until the top gives way and the insides are lightly crushed. Rotate the pan 90 degrees and mash the potatoes again more forcefully, until they are

*continued*

## Makes 4 servings

**For the pesto tofu:**

¼ cup (about 20 small to medium) roughly chopped garlic cloves

¼ cup finely chopped red onion

¼ cup roughly chopped kalamata olives

4 firmly packed cups fresh parsley leaves (from about 2 medium bunches)

¼ cup fresh oregano leaves

1 cup olive oil

1 tablespoon freshly squeezed lime juice

1 tablespoon red wine vinegar

4 teaspoons paprika

1 tablespoon sugar

1 teaspoon cayenne (optional)

1 teaspoon crushed red pepper flakes

Sea salt

1 to 2 pounds firm or extra-firm tofu (preferably your favorite local brand), cut lengthwise into five ½-inch-thick pieces

Olive oil cooking spray

1 cup Basil-Walnut Pesto (page 9)

For the smashed purple potatoes:

1 pound (about 8) baby purple potatoes

¼ cup plus 3 tablespoons olive oil, divided

3 garlic cloves

Sea salt and freshly ground pepper

2 tablespoons chopped fresh parsley

2 tablespoons chopped fresh chives, rosemary, or thyme

Zest and juice of 1 medium lemon

For the charred asparagus:

1 bunch (1 to 1½ pounds) large asparagus, tough ends trimmed

2 teaspoons chopped garlic

2 tablespoons olive oil

Sea salt and freshly ground pepper

slightly flattened. (The idea is to open up the potato enough to let in the flavors of the garlic and herbs.) Brush the tops of each crushed potato generously with the remaining 3 tablespoons of oil and sprinkle with the garlic. Season to taste with salt and pepper. Bake the potatoes until they're golden brown, 20 to 25 minutes. Remove the pan from the oven and sprinkle the potatoes with the parsley, chives, and lemon zest and juice. Set aside.

To make the asparagus, in a large bowl or on a baking sheet, toss the asparagus with the garlic and oil. Season to taste with salt and pepper.

Heat a stovetop or outdoor grill to high heat. Grill the asparagus for 1 to 3 minutes on each side, until they are bright green and still have a crunch.

Heat a medium sauté pan or stovetop griddle over medium heat. Remove the tofu slices from the marinade with a slotted spatula, reserving the marinade for later use. Working in batches, cook the tofu for 3 to 4 minutes on each side, until they're heated through and crispy on the outside.

To serve, stack 2 potatoes near the center of each of 4 plates. Lean 2 tofu pieces against them, drizzle the tofu with pesto , and arrange 3 to 4 asparagus spears against the tofu.

# Hazelnut Tofu and Tempeh with Millet and Blueberry Salad

Playing around, I invented this protein-rich dish with an attractive appearance and extraordinary flavors. The hazelnut milk sauce gives it a creamy taste, while Pernod, an anise-flavored liqueur, lends an aromatic finish and augments the fresh fennel fronds and bulb. It's not a sweet dish, despite the blueberries, but it's intriguing and rich. Note that it's best to allow time to marinate the tofu overnight.

---

To make the tofu and tempeh, combine the hazelnut milk, oil, parsley, Pernod, fennel seeds, lemon juice, fennel bulb and fronds, red pepper flakes, garlic, and onion in a large bowl. Season to taste with salt and pepper. Pour about ½ cup of this marinade into a shallow, medium baking pan, place the tempeh and tofu pieces on top, and cover with the remaining marinade. Cover and refrigerate. After 6 to 8 hours, remove the tempeh with a slotted spoon and transfer to a covered dish (it will taste bitter if it marinates too long), but leave the tofu to marinate overnight.

To make the salad, bring a large pot of salted boiling water (holding at least 8 cups) to a boil. Add the millet and boil until the kernels soften and plump, about 20 minutes. Drain the millet through a fine mesh strainer. Heat the oil in a medium sauté pan, add the garlic, and cook until golden brown, about 1 to 2 minutes. Add the millet, stock, and parsley, and toss. Let the water evaporate and turn off the heat. Add the blueberries and season to taste with salt and pepper. Set aside.

To make the sauce, heat 2 tablespoons of the oil in a medium skillet over medium heat. Add the seitan and fennel and cook until slightly browned, 1 to 2 minutes. Add the red pepper flakes, lemon juice, hazelnut milk, and parsley, and season to taste with salt and pepper. Turn off the heat but leave the skillet on the burner. Add the buttery spread and stir until it melts and incorporates into the sauce.

Heat the remaining 3 tablespoons of oil in a large skillet over medium-high heat. Remove the tofu from the marinade with a slotted spatula. Working in batches, cook the tofu and tempeh pieces for about 4 minutes, until they begin to brown and crisp, then flip them carefully

## Makes 4 servings

For the hazelnut tofu and tempeh:

2 cups unflavored hazelnut milk (such as Pacific brand)

⅔ cup olive oil

¼ cup loosely packed chopped fresh parsley, both leaves and stems

¼ cup Pernod

2 teaspoons fennel seeds, lightly crushed

⅔ cup freshly squeezed lemon juice (from 4 medium lemons)

½ medium fennel bulb (about 6 ounces), trimmed and cut into ¼-inch matchsticks, reserving ¼ cup for sauce that follows and reserving ¼ cup chopped fronds

1 teaspoon crushed red pepper flakes

6 to 8 Roasted Garlic Cloves (page 10), smashed

¼ cup finely diced white onion

Sea salt and freshly ground pepper

1 pound firm or extra-firm tofu (preferably your favorite local brand), cut lengthwise into five ½-inch-thick pieces

8 ounces soy or multigrain tempeh, cut into four ¼-inch-thick pieces

*continued*

For the millet and
   blueberry salad:

1 cup millet

1 tablespoon olive oil

1 teaspoon chopped garlic

¼ cup vegan vegetable stock
   or water

2 tablespoons chopped
   fresh parsley

¼ cup blueberries

Sea salt and freshly ground
   pepper

For the hazelnut sauce:

5 tablespoons olive oil,
   divided

4 ounces seitan, torn into
   bite-size pieces

4 teaspoons chopped fennel
   bulb

Pinch of crushed red pepper
   flakes

Juice of 1 medium lemon

1 cup unflavored hazelnut
   milk

1½ teaspoons chopped
   parsley, plus extra for
   garnish

Sea salt and freshly ground
   pepper

1 tablespoon vegan buttery
   spread (such as Earth
   Balance brand)

with a spatula so the delicate tofu doesn't tear, and cook for another 2 to 4 minutes on the other side, until browned and crispy.

To serve, place a scoop of the salad in the center of each of 4 plates. Arrange a piece of tofu and tempeh on top, and spoon a few tablespoons of sauce over it all. Garnish with the parsley.

# Tempeh Vermouth

The Vermouth Sauce, our vegan version of a classic butter sauce, is made with traditional techniques. The more rosemary you use, the more aromatic and tasty the sauce will be.

---

Combine the vermouth, garlic, red pepper flakes, rosemary, lemon zest and juice, salt, and soy sauce in a large mixing bowl. Pour about 1½ cups of this marinade into a shallow, medium baking pan, place the tempeh pieces on top, and cover with the remaining marinade. Cover and refrigerate for at least 6 to 12 hours, or overnight for a stronger flavor.

Film the bottom of a medium skillet with oil and heat the oil over medium heat. Remove the tempeh from the marinade with a slotted spatula, and, working in batches, cook the pieces for about 4 minutes on each side, or until browned and slightly crispy and heated through.

To serve, arrange 2 pieces of tempeh in the center of each of 4 plates and pour ¼ cup sauce over the top.

**Makes 4 servings**

3 cups dry vermouth

3 tablespoons chopped garlic

1 tablespoon crushed red pepper flakes

3 tablespoons chopped fresh rosemary

Zest and juice of 2 medium lemons

1½ tablespoons sea salt

3 tablespoons gluten-free soy sauce

4 (8-ounce) packages soy or multigrain tempeh, blocks halved lengthwise to make four ¼-inch-thick pieces

Olive oil, for frying

1 cup Vermouth Sauce (recipe follows)

## Vermouth Sauce (SF/GF)

Heat the oil in a medium sauté pan over medium-high heat. Add the garlic, olives, and rosemary (or more to taste), and cook until browned, 1 to 2 minutes. Add the red pepper flakes and carefully pour in the vermouth—if you're cooking on a gas range, it may flame up. Simmer for 3 to 5 minutes, then add the lemon juice (or more to taste) and season to taste with salt and pepper. Turn off the heat but leave the pan on the burner. Quickly stir in the buttery spread until it melts and incorporates into the sauce.

**Makes about 1 cup**

1 tablespoon olive oil

4 Roasted Garlic Cloves (page 10)

½ cup chopped pitted olives, preferably kalamata or Niçoise

1 tablespoon fresh rosemary leaves

Pinch of crushed red pepper flakes

1 cup dry vermouth

1 teaspoon freshly squeezed lemon juice

Sea salt and freshly ground pepper

2 tablespoons vegan buttery spread (such as Earth Balance brand)

# Apple Tempeh Fillets

There's no sweetness to this light, fresh dish; the fennel acts as a subtle helper to place it firmly on the savory side. For those interested in cooking seasonally, good storage methods have made local apples almost always crisp and available. The marinade penetrates the tempeh and gives it a slightly earthy, crisp, and aromatic flavor from the apple fennel. I like this tempeh with Roasted Yam Ravioli with Chantrelle Cream Sauce (page 98), or for a lighter meal, serve with Quinoa-Millet Cherry Salad (page 30); it makes this dish the perfect goodbye to winter and hello to spring.

---

Combine the marinade ingredients in a large bowl. Pour about a quarter of the marinade into a shallow, medium baking pan, place the tempeh pieces on top, and cover with the remaining marinade. Cover and refrigerate for 4 to 6 hours, or overnight for a stronger flavor.

When you're ready to serve the tempeh, heat the oil in a large sauté pan or stovetop griddle over medium heat. Cook the tempeh pieces in 2 batches, until they're golden brown and crisp around the edges, 2 to 4 minutes on each side.

**Makes 1 pound**

For the marinade:

1 cup olive oil

1 cup apple cider

1 medium-size Fuji apple (or substitute your favorite variety), peeled, cored, and cut into matchsticks

¼ cup freshly squeezed lemon juice (from 2 medium lemons)

1 tablespoon apple cider vinegar

¼ cup chopped fresh chives

½ small fennel bulb (about 4 ounces), trimmed and cut into ¼-inch matchsticks, 1 tablespoon chopped fronds reserved

2 tablespoons finely chopped fresh dill

2 tablespoons finely chopped fresh mint

2 teaspoons finely chopped garlic

For the tempeh:

1 tablespoon canola oil

1 pound soy or multigrain tempeh, cut into eight ¼-inch-thick pieces

# Chimichurri Seitan Steaks

**Makes 4 servings**

3 tablespoons chopped garlic

2 tablespoons chopped yellow onion

2 cups firmly packed fresh parsley or cilantro leaves (from about 2 medium bunches parsley or 2 medium bunches cilantro)

2 tablespoons chopped kalamata olives

¼ cup fresh oregano leaves

½ cup plus 1 tablespoon olive oil, divided

2 tablespoons red wine vinegar

1 tablespoon freshly squeezed lime juice

½ teaspoon crushed red pepper flakes

2 teaspoons paprika

Sea salt

1 pound seitan, sliced into four 1- to 1½-inch-thick pieces

Olives, citrus, and fresh herbs add deep, zingy flavors to seitan, giving it a punch it doesn't usually possess. I like serving this with charred asparagus (see Pesto Tofu with Smashed Purple Potatoes and Charred Asparagus, page 73) and grilled onions. Pair it with a mild side such as smashed potatoes or couscous. If you can't find seitan sold in blocks, it's OK to use precut chunks or strips.

---

Put the garlic and onions in the bowl of a food processor and pulse until finely minced. Add the parsley, olives, and oregano, and pulse briefly until they are finely chopped. It is important to stop before the mixture turns into a smooth puree. Or, to make by hand, mince all ingredients with a sharp knife and combine in a small mixing bowl. Scrape the mixture into a medium bowl. Stir in ½ cup of the oil, vinegar, lime juice, red pepper flakes, and paprika. (Note: Adding the liquids outside the food processor gives the marinade the correct texture; again, you don't want the herbs to be processed to the point where they're completely pureed.) Season to taste with salt.

Pour about ½ cup of the marinade into a medium baking dish and add the seitan pieces, rolling to coat them evenly. Spread the remaining marinade over the top. Cover and refrigerate for 6 to 8 hours, or overnight.

Heat the remaining 1 tablespoon oil in a large skillet over medium-high heat. Remove the seitan pieces from the marinade, scraping off any large chunks of herbs that might burn. Cook them for about 2 to 4 minutes on each side, flipping them carefully with a spatula, until they're browned and cooked through.

# Oregano and Parsley Grilled Seitan Steaks

This recipe is similar to Chimichurri Seitan Steaks (page 80), but the marinade gives the seitan a lighter, brighter, more summery flavor. I like serving it with summer squash prepared with salt, pepper, olive oil, and a little thyme or garlic, and then grilled on an outside grill, and Lemon Dill Aioli (page 25), but it would go well with any of our small plates.

---

Heat a stovetop or outdoor grill to high heat.

Spray the seitan pieces evenly with the cooking spray on both sides. Grill for about 1 minute on each side, or until distinct hash marks form.

Add the garlic to taste to the bowl of a food processor and pulse until finely chopped. Add the parsley and oregano, and pulse briefly, until they are also finely chopped. Or, mince all ingredients by hand with a sharp knife. Transfer the mixture to a small bowl. Add ½ cup of the oil, vinegar, red pepper flakes, cumin, salt, and pepper, and stir. (Note: Adding the liquids outside the food processor gives the marinade the correct texture; you don't want the herbs to be processed to the point where they're completely pureed.)

Pour about ½ cup of the marinade into a medium baking dish and add the seitan pieces, rolling to coat them evenly. Spread the remaining marinade over the top. Cover and refrigerate for 6 to 8 hours, or overnight.

Heat the remaining 1 tablespoon of oil in a large skillet over medium-high heat. Remove the seitan pieces from the marinade, scraping off any large chunks of herbs that might burn. Cook them for about 2 to 4 minutes, on each side, flipping them carefully with a spatula, until they're browned and cooked through.

**Makes 4 servings**

1 pound seitan, sliced into four 1- to 1½-inch-thick pieces

Olive oil cooking spray

Garlic

1 cup packed fresh Italian parsley

¼ cup loosely packed oregano leaves

½ cup plus 1 tablespoon olive oil, divided

⅓ cup red wine vinegar

½ teaspoon crushed red pepper flakes

1½ teaspoons ground cumin

½ teaspoon sea salt

½ teaspoon freshly ground pepper

# Transitional Raw

Raw food diets, in which none of your food can be heated above 118 degrees F, can be a great health benefit, but they're not for everyone. They don't allow for a lot of leeway and require serious equipment such as dehydrators and heavy-duty juicers. I like making "transitional" raw recipes instead. They still don't call for much heat and are delicious whether or not you're preparing to take a complete plunge into a raw diet. They're a good bridge for both the digestive system and the mind: they get your body accustomed to eating foods that are mainly uncooked, and mentally they get you in the habit of eating dishes that are room temperature or cold, which can feel strange at first.

All that aside, I also just enjoy the variety and change of pace that comes from preparing foods like "raviolis" made from vegetables and tostadas with fruit.

# Raw "Lasagna" with Basil-Walnut Pesto

**Makes 4 servings**

Six 6-inch sprouted grain tortillas (such as Ezekiel 4:9 brand), halved

½ cup Basil Soy Ricotta (page 8)

2 English cucumbers, left unpeeled and thinly sliced

2 tomatoes, sliced about ⅛ inch thick

16 large fresh basil leaves

Sea salt and freshly ground pepper

½ cup Basil-Walnut Pesto (page 9)

¼ cup pitted kalamata olives, for garnish

I switch to a raw food diet for Lent every year, and I crave something more than salads. I don't have a dehydrator, and I have a severe allergy to Brazil nuts, a key ingredient in many raw dishes, so one year I developed this "lasagna" as a staple dish, using whole-grain tortillas in place of pasta. It has the look of regular layered lasagna, but a very different texture and taste.

---

Place a tortilla half on each of 4 plates. Spread each with about 2 teaspoons of soy ricotta. Layer 3 slices of cucumber over the ricotta, then 2 slices of tomato, then a basil leaf. Season to taste with salt and pepper, then lay down another tortilla half and repeat the process until you have 3 stacked layers with a final tortilla half on top. Spoon a dollop of walnut pesto on the side and garnish the pesto with a few olives.

# Kale Pesto "Pizza"

I like to use sprouted grain tortillas for these protein- and vegetable-packed "pizzas." They don't technically count toward an all-raw diet, but they're still cooked at lower temperatures than traditional breads, and, along with the all-raw toppings, they offer nutritional benefits. Note that the kale isn't stemmed here. Beyond cutting off bruised bottoms, I don't stem my kale, or my herbs and greens, for any recipe, because most of the flavor is in the stem. My goal with food is zero waste.

---

Spread 1 to 2 tablespoons of the walnut pesto on each tortilla.

In a small bowl, season the kale with salt and pepper to taste, tossing so that it's evenly covered.

Layer some kale on top of the pesto, put a few tomato strips on the kale, and top with 1 to 2 tablespoons of tofu relish.

**Makes 4 servings**

½ cup Basil-Walnut Pesto (page 9)

Four 6-inch sprouted grain tortillas (such as Ezekiel 4:9 brand)

2 large kale leaves, sliced into thin ribbons (1 cup)

Sea salt and freshly ground pepper

½ cup sun-dried tomatoes in oil, cut into thin strips

½ cup Raw Tofu Relish (page 11)

# Raw Tostadas with Spicy Strawberry Avocado Salad and Cilantro Relish (GF)

Strawberries make a sweet splash against the spicy jalapeño and cooling jicama in this recipe, standing in for more traditional tostada flavors like avocado and lime. The raw tortillas make for a different texture than the usual crisped version, one that's fun to try out.

Mix the strawberries, jicama, cilantro, jalapeño, lime juice, and avocados in a large bowl. Season to taste with salt and pepper.

Place a tortilla on each of 4 plates and spoon ¾ to 1 cup of the strawberry mixture on top. Sprinkle with the paprika and cumin. Add 1 tablespoon of cilantro relish to each. Top with a cilantro sprig and a lime wedge.

**Makes 4 servings**

1 pound strawberries, hulled and halved (or quartered, if large)

8 ounces jicama, peeled and diced (about 1 cup)

½ cup chopped fresh cilantro, both stems and leaves

1 teaspoon minced jalapeño

Juice of 1 medium lime

2 medium avocados, peeled, seeded, and diced

Sea salt and freshly ground pepper

Four 6-inch raw sprouted corn tortillas (such as Ezekiel 4:9 brand)

⅛ teaspoon paprika

⅛ teaspoon ground cumin (optional)

¼ cup Cilantro Soy Relish (recipe follows)

4 sprigs fresh cilantro

1 lime, cut into 4 wedges

## Cilantro Soy Relish

**Makes about 1 pound**

2 pounds silken firm or regular tofu (preferably your favorite local brand), drained

1 teaspoon ground coriander

½ teaspoon chopped garlic

1 teaspoon sea salt

1 teaspoon pepper

¼ cup olive oil

2 teaspoons evaporated cane juice

2 tablespoons freshly squeezed lime juice (from 1 medium lime)

¼ cup fresh cilantro, cut into ribbons

Crumble the tofu into bead-size pieces. Mix it with the coriander, garlic, salt, pepper, oil, cane juice, lime juice (or more to taste), and cilantro in a medium bowl until it has a chunky, relish-like consistency.

# Jicama Avocado "Ravioli" with Peach and Watermelon Salsa (GF)

**Makes 4 to 6 servings**

**For the ravioli:**

1 teaspoon freshly squeezed lemon juice

1 medium (12 ounce) jicama, peeled and sliced paper thin

1½ avocados, peeled and pitted

½ teaspoon minced garlic

1 teaspoon freshly squeezed lime juice

½ cup Raw Tofu Relish (page 11)

Paprika, for seasoning

Sea salt and freshly ground pepper

**For the salsa:**

1 small serrano or jalapeño pepper, minced

Zest and juice of 2 medium limes

1 cup diced seedless yellow watermelon

2 small ripe peaches, peeled and diced (about 1 cup)

¼ cup chopped fresh basil

¼ cup chopped fresh chives

4 ounces colorful baby heirloom tomatoes, halved (or quartered if large)

Sea salt and freshly ground pepper

6 sprigs fresh basil, for garnish

Jicama is technically a root vegetable, but I think of it as being in the watermelon family, with its fresh, juicy crunch. It's underused, maybe because people find it hard to figure out how to handle the slight spicy edge that's also part of its nature. I use it in this raw "ravioli," matching its sharpness with paprika and lime, then offsetting it with a cool, sweet salsa made from peaches and watermelon.

---

To make the ravioli, pour the lemon juice into a large bowl of water. Soak the jicama slices in the acidulated water until you're ready to use them, to keep them from browning.

Mash the avocados, garlic, and lime juice together in a medium bowl. Add the tofu relish and gently mix. Season to taste with the paprika, salt, and pepper.

To make the salsa, whisk the serrano and lime zest and juice in a large bowl. Fold in the watermelon, peaches, basil, chives, and tomatoes, and season to taste with salt and pepper.

To serve, drain the jicama. Put a round on each serving plate, spoon 1 teaspoon of the avocado mixture in the middle, and top with another jicama slice. Repeat with the remaining jicama; you should have 3 or 4 raviolis per plate. Top with 1 or 2 spoonfuls of salsa. Garnish with the basil sprigs and serve immediately.

# Pasta

Dried pasta is fine most of the time, as in Plum's Smoky Mac (page 101), but sometimes there's no comparison to the lightness and bite of homemade fresh pasta. It's fun to make too. Like pie dough, pasta dough has a finicky reputation, but once you fool around with it and adjust it to your liking, it's not hard—and it's not hard to make a vegan version once you figure out the logistics. Ours was a success when I developed a vegan "egg foam" that's about as good a substitute as I think you can get for the binding and textural qualities of eggs.

# Fresh Spinach Pasta (SF)

Think of this as egg-white pasta. This recipe was so easy, I even surprised myself—I fell so in love with it that I added a complete handmade pasta section to Plum's menu.

Take your time, experiment, and trust your instincts. In time you'll be able to tell if the dough needs more water or more flour or feels just right.

Our Green Egg Foam, made with wilted spinach, gives this pasta a lovely grassy-green color, though you won't notice the spinach taste in the noodles.

**Makes about 14 ounces**

2 cups "00" flour, plus more for flouring work surface

½ cup Green Egg Foam (page 3)

1 tablespoon olive oil

Pinch of sea salt

2 teaspoons water

---

Prepare your work surface by sprinkling it with flour.

Put the flour, green egg foam, oil, and salt in the bowl of a food processor. With the machine running, drizzle in the water. The mixture will first look flaky and then start to come together into a dough. Stop the processor after about 1 minute, when the dough is slightly crumbly but holds together when you press it between your fingers.

Set the dough on the floured work surface and knead it for a few minutes, forming a smooth round ball. (It should be tacky to the touch. If it crosses the line into stickiness, add more flour, 1 tablespoon at a time. Conversely, if it's dry and won't hold together, add water 1 tablespoon at a time.)

Wrap the dough ball in plastic wrap and let it rest in the refrigerator for about 1 hour. (If you're rolling the pasta by hand, let it rest on the counter instead of in the fridge; it'll be easier to handle.)

Cut the dough in half and flatten each half with a rolling pin. Using a pasta machine or a stand mixer's pasta attachment, roll it through a few times on the thickest setting. If the dough is sticking, add a bit more flour. When it holds together in a well-shaped rectangle and is flattened to about ¼ inch, turn up the settings according to your machine's directions for ravioli and fettuccini (I use setting #4 on my KitchenAid attachment) and continue rolling it through to the thickness you want. Repeat with the other half of the dough.

If you're rolling the dough by hand, put the chunk of dough between 2 pieces of wax paper and roll it with a pin until it's as thin as possible without breaking—less than 1/16 inch thick.

*continued*

To make noodles, with a sharp knife or using your machine's noodle attachment, slice the pasta into even strips the width you like (⅜ inch is standard for fettuccini). Leave it in whole sheets for ravioli and other filled pastas. Lay the pasta flat on a parchment-lined baking tray and let it dry for about 1 hour. Store flat sheets of pasta between layers of wax paper or parchment paper. To store cut noodles, dust them with flour and bundle them into covered Tupperware containers. The pasta will keep for 2 to 3 days in the refrigerator.

## Tips on making vegan pasta

For flour, I prefer soft, finely ground Italian "00" flour, which is available at specialty markets and online, or close substitutes such as King Arthur's Italian-style flour. It's OK to substitute all-purpose flour if you want; even famed Italian cookbook author Marcella Hazan makes her pasta that way.

You can make the recipe gluten-free by using a gluten-free all-purpose flour; gluten-free dough will be a bit more gummy, but still good. If you're making gluten-free pasta, you can skip the step where the dough rests, because this step activates the gluten in the dough.

# Handmade Linguini in Sauvignon Blanc Cream Sauce with King Trumpet Mushroom "Scallops"

You'll be the star of dinner with this fancy white-sauce pasta starring firm, elegant king trumpet mushrooms, whose stems have a strikingly scallop-like look and texture when sliced. It's just the sort of dish that's our signature at Plum—a rich, decadent vegan entrée you usually can't find in an upscale restaurant. To make the recipe soy-free, substitute 2 teaspoons of salt for the soy sauce and use Savory Rice Cream (page 7) in place of the cream sauce. King trumpets are cultivated year-round but are sometimes sold under other names, such as king oyster or eryngii mushrooms.

Make the marinade by combining the sauvignon blanc, garlic, red pepper flakes, rosemary, lemon zest and juice, salt, and soy sauce in a large bowl. Add the mushrooms, coating them evenly. Marinate for at least 15 minutes, or longer for a stronger flavor.

Meanwhile fill a large pot with 8 cups of water, salted until it tastes like seawater (about 2 tablespoons of salt). Set it on high heat to boil. Add the linguini and cook until it's al dente, 3 to 5 minutes. Drain and set aside.

Preheat the oven to 350 degrees F.

To make the sauce, heat 1 tablespoon of the oil in a large sauté pan or cast-iron skillet over medium heat. Add the garlic, olives, and 1 tablespoon of the rosemary leaves, and cook until the garlic starts to brown, 1 to 2 minutes. Add the red pepper flakes and carefully pour in the wine—if you're cooking on a gas range, it may flame up. Take care not to let the flames leap into the pan; they will darken the sauce. Simmer for 1 minute, then add the lemon juice and soy cream, and season to taste with salt and pepper. Whisk the sauce to remove any lumps. Add the pasta to the cream sauce and reduce the heat to medium-low.

**Makes 4 servings**

For the mushroom marinade:

1 cup sauvignon blanc

1 tablespoon chopped garlic

½ tablespoon crushed red pepper flakes

1 tablespoon chopped fresh rosemary leaves

Zest and juice of 1 medium lemon

1½ teaspoons sea salt

1 tablespoon soy sauce

8 ounces king trumpet mushrooms, cut into 1½-inch-thick pieces

10 ounces Fresh Spinach Pasta (page 93), cut into linguini

For the cream sauce:

4 tablespoons olive oil, divided

4 Roasted Garlic Cloves (page 10), chopped

½ cup pitted olives, preferably kalamata or Niçoise, roughly chopped

1 tablespoon chopped fresh rosemary leaves, plus extra for garnish

Pinch of crushed red pepper flakes

¼ cup sauvignon blanc

2 tablespoons freshly squeezed lemon juice (from 1 medium lemon)

2 cups Savory Soy Cream (page 6)

Sea salt and freshly ground pepper

*continued*

Heat the remaining 3 tablespoons of the oil in a medium ovenproof frying pan over medium heat. Sear the marinated mushrooms until they turn golden, 2 to 3 minutes on each side. Transfer the pan to the oven and bake the mushrooms for about 5 minutes, until they are softened and done through. Carefully remove the pan from the oven (remember, the handle will be extremely hot) and set aside.

Check the seasonings and add more salt and pepper if needed. When the sauce has thickened, about 2 minutes, remove the pan from the heat.

To serve, divide the pasta among 4 shallow bowls. Top with the mushrooms and garnish with rosemary and more pepper.

# Roasted Yam Ravioli with Apple Tempeh Fillets and Chanterelle Cream Sauce

**Makes 4 servings**

4 sheets Fresh Spinach Pasta (page 93), about 5 to 6 inches wide by 14 to 15 inches long

Flour, for dusting the work surface and pan

1 cup Roasted Yam Mash (recipe follows)

Olive oil, for boiling the pasta

¾ cup Chanterelle Cream Sauce (recipe follows)

8 cooked Apple Tempeh Fillets (page 79)

Apple slices, for garnish

I wanted to try out pastas with really interesting fillings and came up with this version of a rich, earthy apple tempeh dish we serve at Plum. This dish is more substantial and filling when you add the tempeh, but if you don't have time, the pasta and sauce alone taste great. You can use leftovers from the Chai-Spiced Yam Bruschetta with Crunchy Kale (page 52) instead of making the yam mash. And, for a completely stripped-down version, you can use store-bought pasta and just add the sauce. Note that it's best to make the sauce immediately before you plan to use it.

---

Lay a pasta sheet flat on a lightly floured work surface. Gently spoon about 1 tablespoon of the yam mash in a zigzag pattern down the length of the sheet, leaving an inch or 2 between each mound. Brush water on the edges of the sheet to help seal the pasta. Drape a second sheet of pasta loosely over the top of the filling. Using your fingers, gently press around each mound; this will both press out any air bubbles and seal the pasta sheets. Use a little water to help with the seal.

Shape the ravioli by pressing down around the filling with the dull side of a square or round cookie cutter, then cutting them out with the sharp end of the cutter or with a sharp knife. Repeat with the remaining pasta sheets and filling. Each set of pasta sheets should yield 8 ravioli, and there should be about a ¾-inch border around the filling. (You can collect the dough scraps afterward, reroll them, and make some extra ravioli if you like.) Line a baking sheet with wax paper, dust it with flour, place the ravioli in a single layer on the sheet, and refrigerate until ready to use. It will keep in the refrigerator 3 to 5 days or frozen for later use.

When you're ready to cook the ravioli, bring a large pot of water with of pinch of salt added to a gentle boil over medium-high heat. Add a little oil and cook the ravioli until al dente, about 8 minutes. Gently remove the ravioli with a slotted spoon and divide them among 4 fancy serving bowls.

Pour 3 tablespoons of sauce on top of the ravioli in each bowl, layering with 2 pieces of apple tempeh. Garnish with the apple slices.

# Roasted Yam Mash (SF/GF)

Preheat the oven to 400 degrees F and line a baking sheet with aluminum foil or parchment paper for easy cleanup.

Halve the yams lengthwise, put them on the prepared baking sheet, and drizzle with the olive oil. Bake the yams for 45 minutes, or until they're super soft.

Heat the canola oil in a medium sauté pan over medium heat. Add the ginger and garlic and sauté until they're browned, about 2 minutes, stirring occasionally to avoid burning them.

Put the roasted yams in a medium bowl and mash them with the sautéed ginger and garlic, along with the oil they were cooked in. Season to taste with salt and pepper. Mix in the sugar (or more to taste) and buttery spread, and stir until thoroughly combined.

**Makes 3 ½ cups**

2¼ pounds (about 3 medium) red-skinned yams, peeled

1 to 2 tablespoons olive oil

¼ cup canola oil

2 tablespoons chopped peeled fresh ginger (from about a 2-inch piece)

2 tablespoons chopped garlic

Sea salt and freshly ground pepper

1 tablespoon sugar

¼ cup (½ stick) vegan buttery spread (such as Earth Balance brand), melted

# Chanterelle Cream Sauce (SF/GF)

Heat the oil in a large skillet over medium-high heat. Add the garlic and cook until it's golden brown, about 1 minute. Add the chanterelles and cook for about 1 minute, until golden brown, then stir in the fennel, mint, dill, lemon juice, salt, and pepper. Add the apple cider and soy milk, mixing well.

Reduce the heat to medium-low and let the sauce simmer for about 3 minutes until it slightly reduces. Turn the heat to low, add the buttery spread, and stir until it's completely melted and incorporated. Serve immediately.

**Makes about ¾ cup sauce**

2 tablespoons olive oil

1 teaspoon chopped garlic

2 to 3 ounces chanterelle or oyster mushrooms, pulled apart into bite-size pieces

2 teaspoons chopped fennel fronds

1 teaspoon finely chopped fresh mint leaves

1 teaspoon finely chopped fresh dill

1 to 2 teaspoons freshly squeezed lemon juice

1 teaspoon sea salt

1 teaspoon freshly ground pepper

¼ cup apple cider

½ cup unsweetened soy milk

2 tablespoons vegan buttery spread (such as Earth Balance brand)

# Plum's Smoky Mac

At Plum, most of the attention goes to our "Mac 'n' Yease," a vegan mac 'n' cheese from the heavens, with super-secret ingredients. I agree that the Mac 'n' Yease should be on everyone's bucket list, but I'm also a fan of this smoky, creamy pasta made with vegan mozzarella and cheddar and our own smoked tofu. You can't have too many macs in your repertoire.

To make the pasta, bring a large pot of water and the salt to a boil over high heat. Add the macaroni and cook according to the package instructions, until al dente. Drain and set aside.

Preheat the oven to 400 degrees F.

In a medium sauté pan heat the oil over medium heat. Add the tofu and cook until crispy, about 2 to 4 minutes. Put the onion, garlic, and thyme leaves in the same pan and cook for about 5 minutes, or until the onion is soft. Season to taste with salt and pepper. Remove the pan from the heat and set aside.

To make the sauce, in a small saucepan over medium heat, heat the milk with the thyme and garlic until hot but not boiling, about 7 minutes. Strain out the solids using a fine-mesh sieve and set the milk aside.

Melt the buttery spread in a deep sauté pan or Dutch oven over medium-low heat. Whisk in the flour and cook for about 1 minute, stirring constantly. Make sure this roux doesn't darken; turn down the heat if it's in danger of browning.

Whisk the milk into the roux. Continue to whisk over medium-low heat until the roux is smooth, about 1 minute more. Stir in the soy cream until it is thoroughly incorporated, about 1 minute. Season to taste with salt and pepper, and remove the pan from the heat.

Add the cooked macaroni, 4 cups of the cheese, and the red pepper flakes, and fold together until the macaroni is coated. Scrape the mac into a large baking dish (3 quarts is about right, or use 2 smaller dishes). Sprinkle the remaining 1 cup of cheese and tofu-onion mixture over the top, then dust with the panko. Bake until the mac is bubbly in the center, crispy on top, and heated through, about 30 minutes.

## Makes 6 to 8 servings

For the pasta:

2 teaspoons sea salt

1 pound elbow macaroni

1 tablespoon canola oil

3 ounces smoked tofu (such as Baba's Mesquite Tofu), minced to resemble bacon bits

1 large onion, diced

2 teaspoons chopped garlic

2 tablespoons fresh thyme leaves

Sea salt and freshly ground pepper

For the sauce:

3 cups unsweetened soy milk

4 to 6 sprigs fresh thyme

4 garlic cloves, peeled and smashed

3 tablespoons unsalted vegan buttery spread (such as Earth Balance brand)

3 tablespoons all-purpose flour

1 cup Savory Soy Cream (page 7)

Sea salt and freshly ground pepper

5 cups (22.5 ounces) shredded vegan mozzarella or cheddar cheese (such as Daiya brand), divided

2 teaspoons crushed red pepper flakes

½ cup panko (Japanese bread crumbs)

# Grains

The world of grains is so much broader than rice and wheat, and trying out different varieties can add new dimensions to meals. Quinoa comes in brilliant colors and gets a decent amount of attention these days as "the perfect protein," but I prefer millet. It has a milder flavor and can be blended with more ingredients, almost like couscous. I just find it tastier. Then there are heartier grains such as rye berries, which have a wonderful, nice, nutty texture and add good depth to food. The choice depends on what you're cooking—to me grains are not interchangeable—but it's fun to try them all.

# Millet-Stuffed Baby Pumpkins

**Makes 4 servings**

4 baby pumpkins, any variety with sweet flesh and edible skin (such as Baby Bear)

Olive oil cooking spray

1 to 2 tablespoons olive oil

2 teaspoons chopped garlic

8 ounces oyster mushrooms, cleaned and cut into bite-size pieces

¼ pound cherry tomatoes, halved or quartered if large

8 ounces baked soy or multigrain tempeh, crumbled

2 cups cooked millet

2 cups vegan chicken stock (such as Imagine brand)

4 large kale leaves, stemmed and chopped (about 2 cups)

2 tablespoons chopped fresh basil

2 tablespoons chopped fresh parsley

Sea salt and freshly ground pepper

Baby pumpkins are adorable and festive and thoroughly seasonal, usually available only during the fall harvest. Think about making this dish for a vegan Thanksgiving celebration or dinner party. The only real trick is to keep an eye out as the pumpkins bake so they are tender and yet not falling apart. To add a fancier touch, use the pumpkin seeds as a garnish: rinse them and toss in olive oil and salt, then toast them on a baking sheet at 375 degrees F until they're crunchy.

---

Preheat the oven to 400 degrees F and line a baking sheet with aluminum foil or parchment paper for easy cleanup.

Carefully cut the tops off the pumpkins with a sharp paring knife and scoop out and discard the seeds. Spray the pumpkins with the cooking spray inside and out. Bake them on the prepared baking sheet until fork-tender, about 20 minutes. Place on individual plates and set aside.

Meanwhile, in a large sauté pan, heat the oil over medium-high heat. Add the garlic and sauté until brown, about 1 minute. Add the mushrooms and cook until they release their liquid, about another minute. Add the tomatoes, tempeh, millet, and stock, stirring to incorporate. Add the kale, basil, and parsley, and let the stuffing steam 1 minute until the kale is just barely tender. Season to taste with salt and pepper.

Stuff each pumpkin with about ¾ cup of filling until it generously spills over the top.

# Grilled Spelt Crust Pizza with Pears and Ricotta

During my career I have had some adventurous personal chef gigs. I developed this pizza during one of my favorites, with actor/musician Common. He loves pizza, especially spelt, so I came up with this earthy early-fall recipe.

Grilling pizza dough might sound unusual, but it's an impressively easy way to ensure a crisp crust. The dough may sag when you first transfer it to the hot grill, but it firms up almost immediately. Spelt flour gives this pizza a nutty flavor and a pleasant, slightly gritty texture.

This recipe makes two pizza crusts. One can be frozen after grilling. If tightly wrapped in plastic, it will keep in the freezer about one week.

---

Preheat a gas or stovetop grill to medium heat. Brush the pears and onions with the oil, and season lightly with salt and pepper. Put them on the grill and close the lid. Cook for 1 minute or so, until grill marks are visible, and flip using tongs or a spatula. Grill the other side until the bottoms are marked and softened, about 3 minutes total. Remove from the grill and set aside on a plate.

Place the pizza crust on a baking sheet so it will be easier to transfer to the grill. Spread the pesto over the top. Sprinkle evenly with the ricotta and mozzarella cheeses, and top with the grilled pears and onions. Slide the pizza onto the grill. Close the lid and cook until the cheeses soften, 2 to 4 minutes.

Slide the baking sheet underneath the pizza to remove it from the grill and transfer it to a cutting board. Sprinkle the arugula over the top, slice, and serve immediately.

**Makes one 16-by-6-inch pizza**

2 Bartlett or Bosc pears, cored and cut into ¼-inch-thick slices

½ small red onion, cut into ⅛-inch rounds

Olive oil, for brushing

Sea salt and freshly ground pepper

1 Grilled Spelt Pizza Crust (recipe follows)

¼ cup Basil-Walnut Pesto (page 9)

¼ cup crumbled soy ricotta cheese

2 tablespoons shredded vegan mozzarella cheese (such as Daiya brand)

½ cup lightly packed arugula, tough stems discarded

# Grilled Spelt Pizza Crust

To proof the yeast, put the warm water, yeast, and flour in the bowl of a stand mixer (or in a large bowl). Whisk quickly by hand for 10 seconds. Cover the bowl with plastic wrap and let the yeast stand at room temperature for 30 minutes. It will be bubbly.

To make the dough, when the yeast is fully active, add the cold water, oil, all-purpose and spelt flours, and salt to the bowl. Fit the mixer with the dough hook, fit the bowl to the mixer, and mix the dough on medium speed for about 1½ minutes, or until it pulls away from the sides of the bowl. (If you're mixing by hand, knead for 5 to 7 minutes.) If the dough is sticky, add more spelt flour, 1 tablespoon at a time.

Lightly coat a large bowl with the oil. Coat the dough ball with additional oil and let it rise in the bowl in a warm place, covered, until it doubles in size, which can take as little as 45 minutes.

When the dough has doubled in size, punch it down and form it into a ball again. Cover it with plastic wrap and let it rest for 30 minutes. It will be velvety and pliable.

Preheat a gas or stovetop grill to medium heat.

Using a sharp knife, divide the dough into 2 portions. On a lightly floured surface, roll out each portion with a rolling pin to an uneven rectangle roughly 16 inches long, 6 inches wide, and ¼ inch thick. Transfer the dough to 2 baking sheets.

Working with one crust at a time, brush the dough lightly on both sides with the oil and slide it directly on the grill. Grill the crust, uncovered, until bubbles form on the top and grill marks form on the bottom, about 4 minutes. Flip the crust with tongs, close the lid, and grill until the bottom of the crust is browned, about another 4 minutes. Using tongs or a long metal spatula, transfer the dough back to the baking sheet until it is ready for toppings.

**Makes two 16-by-6-inch pizza crusts**

For proofing the yeast:

½ cup warm water

4 teaspoons instant yeast

½ cup all-purpose flour

For the dough:

¾ cup cold water

¼ cup olive oil, plus extra for coating the bowl and dough

1 cup all-purpose flour, plus extra for flouring the work surface

2½ cups spelt flour

1½ teaspoons sea salt

# Blue Corn Pizza with Pesto-Grilled Heirloom Tomatoes and Ricotta

**Makes 4 personal-size pizzas**

4 firm but ripe medium heirloom tomatoes (about 1½ pounds), cut into uneven pieces (use different colors if you can find them)

Sea salt and freshly ground pepper

2 tablespoons olive oil

4 parbaked Blue Corn Pizza Crusts (recipe follows)

½ cup garlic oil (store-bought, or use leftover oil from Roasted Garlic Cloves, page 10)

½ cup Basil-Walnut Pesto (page 9)

1 cup Basil Soy Ricotta (page 8)

4 Roasted Garlic Cloves (page 10), chopped (optional)

½ cup baby arugula, roughly torn

I developed this pizza while on a gig for Joaquin Phoenix and his family. He's a cool person and a lifelong vegan, and he made it clear that they didn't want any chi-chi vegan food. He said, "I'm going to need something a little heartier." The sweet, finely ground blue cornmeal I use here adds a touch of color and texture to baked goods. The goal here is to have a crust with a slightly uneven shape and thickness. Don't make the range too dramatic, or it won't cook evenly, but a little bit of that rustic look and feel is just what you want. This recipe is also a great place to use ends and uneven scraps of heirloom tomatoes that would otherwise go to waste.

The pizza crusts can be baked in advance and frozen. If tightly wrapped in plastic, they will keep in the freezer about one week.

---

Preheat a gas or stovetop grill to high heat. Season the tomatoes with salt and pepper to taste and toss gently with the oil. Put the tomatoes, cut side down, directly on the grill. Close the lid and cook for 4 to 8 minutes, until they are nicely charred but not smoking. Remove them carefully with a metal spatula and set them aside on a plate.

Preheat the oven to 450 degrees F.

Place the parbaked crusts on 2 baking sheets. Brush them with the garlic oil and spread the walnut pesto over the top, leaving an uneven border roughly 1 inch wide. Arrange the grilled tomatoes on top of each pizza, and dollop the ricotta in the gaps between the tomatoes. Scatter the roasted garlic on top. Bake the pizzas until the edges are crisp, 7 to 10 minutes. Remove the pizzas, sprinkle the arugula over the top, slice, and serve immediately.

# Blue Corn Pizza Crust

To proof the yeast, put the warm water, yeast, and flour in the bowl of a stand mixer (or in a large bowl). Whisk quickly by hand for 10 seconds. Cover the bowl with plastic wrap and let the yeast stand at room temperature for 30 minutes. It should be bubbly.

To make the dough, when the yeast is fully active, add the cold water, oil, cornmeal, flour, and salt to the bowl. Fit the mixer with the dough hook, fit the bowl to the mixer, and mix the dough on medium speed for 1 to 2 minutes, until the dough is smooth and a little tacky to the touch. (If you're mixing it by hand, knead for 5 to 7 minutes.) If the dough is sticky, add more flour, 1 tablespoon at a time. It should pull away from the edge of the bowl.

Lightly coat a large bowl with oil. Coat the dough ball with additional olive oil and let it rise in the bowl in a warm place, covered, until it doubles in size; this may take as little as 45 minutes or as long as 2 hours.

When the dough has doubled in size, punch it down and form it into a ball again. Cover it with plastic wrap and let it rest for 30 minutes.

Preheat the oven to 450 degrees F.

Using a sharp knife, divide the dough into 4 portions. On a lightly floured surface, roll out each portion with a rolling pin to your desired shape and thickness. Sprinkle 1 or 2 baking sheets (depending on the size of your pizzas) with cornmeal to keep the crusts from burning, and place the crusts on them. Bake the crusts until they are firm enough to flip, about 3 minutes, then flip them with tongs or a long spatula and cook them for another 3 to 4 minutes on the other side. (You don't want the crust to be cooked through; it'll go in the oven for one final turn after you add the toppings.) Cool the crusts for 10 to 15 minutes before adding toppings.

Optional step for extra visual appeal: preheat a gas or stovetop grill to 450 degrees F. Spray the crusts with cooking spray and grill them on one side for 3 to 5 minutes, until grill marks form on the bottom. Be careful not to let them burn.

**Makes 4 personal-size pizza crusts**

For proofing the yeast:

½ cup warm water

4 teaspoons instant yeast

½ cup all-purpose flour

For the dough:

¾ cup cold water

¼ cup olive oil, plus extra to coat the bowl and dough

1 cup blue cornmeal, plus extra for sprinkling the baking sheet

2½ cups all-purpose flour, plus extra for flouring the work surface

1½ teaspoons sea salt

# Quinoa Risotto with Panko-Fried Portobellos

**Makes 4 servings**

1 medium (about 2 pounds) butternut squash

½ cup unsweetened soy milk

1 teaspoon white vinegar

1 cup panko (Japanese bread crumbs)

2 large portobello mushrooms, stems and gills removed, sliced into finger-lengths

5 cups vegan chicken stock (such as Imagine brand)

3½ tablespoons extra-virgin olive oil, divided

1½ cups chopped yellow onion

2 large garlic cloves, chopped

4 teaspoons finely chopped fresh thyme, divided

¾ cup red quinoa

½ cup dry white wine

4 cups vegetable oil

½ cup (2 ounces) vegan Parmesan cheese

Sea salt and freshly ground pepper

Fall into autumn with this hearty mix of creamy and crunchy textures and flavors. Butternut squash adds a particularly sweet note here. I adapted the risotto from a more classic Epicurious.com recipe that paired it with shrimp; I can't imagine a better match for it than the crunch of fried mushrooms. I use red quinoa because it is so colorful. If you can't find it, substitute white.

Preheat the oven to 400 degrees F and line a baking sheet with aluminum foil or parchment paper for easy cleanup.

With a knife, pierce the squash in several spots to allow it to release steam while cooking. Place the squash on the prepared baking sheet and bake until fork-tender, about 1 hour. Remove the squash from the oven and let it cool. When it is cool enough to handle, halve the squash, scoop out the seeds and discard, and put the flesh into a blender or the bowl of a food processor. Puree until smooth, and set aside.

In a small bowl, whisk the soy milk and vinegar. Let the mixture sit for 1 to 2 minutes, until it has thickened slightly.

Put the panko in a medium bowl. Coat the mushrooms in the soy milk mixture and toss them in the panko until they are well coated. Set them aside on a plate.

Bring the stock to a simmer over medium-high heat in a medium saucepan, then reduce the heat to low. Keep the stock warm while you sauté the onions and garlic.

In a large saucepan over medium-high heat, heat 2 tablespoons of the olive oil. Add the onions and sauté for 3 to 5 minutes, stirring frequently, until they begin to brown. Add the garlic and 2 teaspoons of the thyme and sauté for about 1 minute more, until the garlic begins to color. Add the quinoa and stir until it is coated. Add the wine and continue stirring until it is almost entirely absorbed by the quinoa; this should take about 3 to 4 minutes. Reduce the heat to medium. Pour in 1 cup of the warm broth and, stirring almost constantly, cook until it is almost entirely absorbed by the quinoa. Repeat the procedure, 1 cup of broth at a time, until the quinoa is just tender but not at all mushy, about 4 to 6 minutes. Turn the heat to low and keep the quinoa warm while you fry the mushrooms.

Heat the vegetable oil in a large, heavy-bottomed Dutch oven to 350 degrees F as measured on an instant-read thermometer. Put the mushrooms in a fry basket, lower it carefully into the hot oil, and cook until they're golden brown, 3 to 7 minutes, depending on their thickness. (If you don't have a fry basket, lower the mushrooms into the oil using a slotted spoon, being careful not to splatter the hot oil.) Carefully remove them with a slotted spoon and put them on a tray or in a bowl lined with paper towels.

Toss the quinoa with 1½ cups of the squash puree, the remaining 2 teaspoons thyme, and the Parmesan. Season to taste with salt and pepper. Top with the fried mushrooms.

# White Bean and Summer Rye Chops Salad with Pesto-Grilled Eggplant (SF)

**Makes 4 servings**

1 large eggplant, cut into ½-inch-thick slices

Sea salt and freshly ground pepper

Canola oil cooking spray

1 cup Basil-Walnut Pesto (page 9), plus extra for topping (optional)

1 cup rye chops

¼ cup olive oil

1 to 2 medium garlic cloves, chopped

1 leek (white and pale green parts only), rinsed well and thinly sliced

1 (12-ounce) can cannellini beans, drained and rinsed

1½ tablespoons freshly squeezed lemon juice (from 1 medium lemon)

¼ cup chopped parsley

This summery salad uses rye chops, a form of cracked and chopped rye berries that can be ordered online from sources such as King Arthur Flour. The cracked "chops" cook faster and more easily than whole berries, and I love their nutty taste. If they aren't readily available, substitute whole rye berries and cook them according to the package directions. Or, to make the dish gluten-free, use millet instead. Note that you'll need to prepare the eggplant at least four to six hours ahead of when you'll be serving. I like to serve this dish with grilled asparagus.

---

Season the eggplant slices lightly with salt and pepper and spray lightly on both sides with the cooking spray. Heat a grill or grill pan to high. Grill the eggplant slices until distinct hatch marks form, 1 to 2 minutes on each side.

Spread the pesto on the bottom of a shallow, large baking pan. Put the grilled eggplant slices in the pan, turning them until they are coated with pesto. Nestle them in the pesto and let them stand covered in the refrigerator for at least 6 to 8 hours, or overnight for a stronger flavor.

Fill a medium saucepan with 6 cups of water. Add a dash of salt and pepper, bring the water to a boil, then reduce the heat to medium-low. Add the rye chops and simmer until tender, 20 to 30 minutes. Drain any remaining water, return the chops to the pan, and set aside.

In a medium sauté pan, heat the oil over medium heat. Add the garlic and sauté for 2 to 3 minutes, until it's golden brown. Add the leeks and cook until they're tender, 2 to 4 minutes. Add the cooked rye chops and the beans, and season with salt and pepper to taste. Stir, add the lemon juice and parsley (or more of both to taste), and remove the pan from the heat.

Spray a sauté pan or stovetop griddle with cooking spray and heat to medium-high. With a spatula, remove the eggplant slices from the pan, making sure some pesto still clings to the slices. Cook the slices for 4 minutes on each side, until they're golden brown and crispy.

To serve, divide the bean salad among 4 plates or big fancy bowls. Lay 2 slices of eggplant on top of each salad and top with a dollop of pesto.

# Desserts

At Plum, we lean toward desserts that use fresh fruits in their whole, organic forms and are simple for the occasional cook to make at home. That's probably because those are the sorts of desserts I prefer myself. My sister is an amazing pastry chef. She'll spend an intimidating three to four hours on layered doughs. But unlike her, I prefer to sauté ripe plums in a white wine sauce, for example, something easy and light I can do on the fly. It's a good fit with the way I eat and with the ingredients themselves. There are times when everyone needs chocolate, of course, but even our chocolate recipes aren't too heavy. We aim for rustic rather than over the top.

# Toasted Chocolate Bread with Cream Cheese Crème Fraîche

This dessert hits all the pleasure centers: it's bread, it's chocolate, it's cream—it's got to be good. Using spelt bread here is a nice way to incorporate whole grains into a dessert in a subtle way that doesn't scream "healthier choice"—even when it is. You can use potato bread or a basic rustic loaf; my favorite is our homemade spelt bread.

---

In a medium saucepan, heat the soy milk over medium heat until it's just boiling. Add the chocolate and turn off the heat, but keep the pot on the burner. Let the sauce stand for about 1 minute, then whisk until smooth. The texture should be thick and rich, just barely pourable. Keep the sauce on the still-warm burner until you're ready to use it.

In a large sauté pan, melt 2 tablespoons of the buttery spread over medium heat. Working in batches, put the bread slices in the pan and toast until golden brown, 1 to 2 minutes on each side. Add more butter as needed.

To serve, overlap 2 slices of toasted bread on each of 4 plates. Pour about 2 tablespoons of chocolate sauce over the bread, aiming for the center where the pieces intersect and letting the sauce cascade down to the plate. Top each with a dollop of crème fraîche and garnish with a sprig of rosemary.

**Makes 4 servings**

½ cup vanilla soy milk

8 ounces dark bittersweet chocolate, finely chopped

3 tablespoons vegan buttery spread (such as Earth Balance brand), softened, divided

8 slices Spelt Bread (recipe follows) or other rustic bread, cut about ½-inch thick

⅓ cup Cream Cheese Crème Fraîche (page 3) or Sweet Soy Cream (page 4)

4 sprigs fresh rosemary, for garnish (optional)

# Spelt Bread

**Makes 2 standard loaves**

**For proofing the yeast:**

1 cup warm water (ideally around 110 degrees F)

1 tablespoon active dry yeast

4 teaspoons dark brown sugar

3 tablespoons olive oil, plus extra to grease pans and hands

**For the dough:**

2 cups spelt flour

1 cup all-purpose flour

2 teaspoons sea salt

To proof the yeast, in a small bowl, combine the warm water, yeast, and brown sugar. Let the mixture sit until large bubbles form on the surface, about 4 to 7 minutes. Mix in the oil.

To make the dough, in a separate large bowl, mix together the spelt and all-purpose flours and salt. When the yeast is fully active, pour it into the dry ingredients. Mix the dough with a soft spatula first, then knead it by hand for about 5 minutes, until the dough forms a neat ball and doesn't stick to your fingers. If it's too sticky, sprinkle it with more spelt flour, a pinch at a time, kneading the flour in.

Leaving the ball of dough in the mixing bowl, cover it with a clean kitchen towel and set it in a warm place (or in the oven at 100 degrees F) until it doubles in size, about 45 minutes. Grease 2 standard loaf pans (ideally 9 by 5 inches) with the oil.

When the dough has doubled, oil your hands and pat down the dough. Divide it into 2 or 3 smaller balls, kneading them slightly and forming them into logs that will fit into the pans. Place the dough in the pans, cover the pans with clean kitchen towels, and return them to a warm spot or the 100-degree oven. Let the dough sit until it doubles in size again, about 30 minutes.

About halfway through the second rise, preheat the oven to 350 degrees F.

Bake the loaves until they make a hollow sound when tapped with a knife and the tops are golden brown, about 30 minutes.

# Sautéed Rosemary Plums with
## White Wine and Blueberry Butter Sauce (GF)

I like to showcase different ways to use our namesake plums. Pairing them with fresh herbs and a white wine sauce makes for a more sophisticated, richer presentation than they get in their typical crisps and crumbles. Use firm plums for this recipe. To make it soy-free, use Sweet Rice Cream (page 8) rather than the soy whipped cream.

**Makes 4 servings**

2 tablespoons vegan buttery spread (such as Earth Balance brand), divided

4 medium plums (about ¾ pound), halved and pitted

¼ cup blueberries, plus a handful for filling the plums

½ cup white wine, preferably chardonnay

1 tablespoon sugar

1 teaspoon freshly squeezed lemon juice (optional)

1 cup store-bought soy whipped cream or Sweet Soy Cream (page 4)

4 sprigs fresh rosemary, for garnish

Melt 1 tablespoon of the buttery spread in a large skillet over medium heat, but not so high that the butter smokes. Sauté the plums for a few minutes, until they blacken slightly but don't burn. Add ¼ cup of the blueberries, wine, sugar, and lemon juice. Reduce the heat to low and simmer the plums until they become tender and the blueberries are slightly broken up, 2 to 3 minutes. Using a slotted spoon, remove the plum halves to a separate plate. Add the remaining 1 tablespoon of buttery spread to the skillet, and stir until the sauce turns opaque.

To serve, put ¼ cup whipped cream on each of 4 plates. Stack 2 plum halves on the cream, then pour 1 to 2 tablespoons of sauce over each. Fill the plum cavities with blueberries and garnish with a sprig of rosemary.

# Oven-Baked Peaches and Cream (GF)

This is another recipe that takes advantage of an abundance of summer peaches. For an elegant presentation, cut a divot in the bottom of each peach after halving them so they have a little kickstand to stand on. This recipe easily doubles; keep in mind that it's hard to stop after just a few bites of ripe peaches. If you want to make it soy-free, substitute Sweet Rice Cream (page 8) for the crème fraîche.

---

Preheat the oven to 450 degrees F.

In a small bowl, mix the cinnamon and sugar. Spray a baking sheet or large baking dish with cooking spray and dab it with the buttery spread. Coat the peach halves with the cinnamon sugar mixture and place them cut side down on the sheet. Drizzle with the peach nectar. Bake the peaches for 10 to 15 minutes, so that they are soft but still hold their shape and have not turned to peach pie.

To serve, place 1 peach half on each plate. Spoon 2 tablespoons of the crème fraîche into the center of each peach, letting it run down the sides. Drizzle with the agave syrup and garnish with the blueberries and a sprig of rosemary.

**Makes 4 servings**

1½ teaspoons ground cinnamon

2 tablespoons sugar

Canola oil cooking spray

1 tablespoon vegan buttery spread (such as Earth Balance brand)

2 large ripe peaches, halved and pitted

¼ cup peach nectar

½ cup Cream Cheese Crème Fraîche (page 3) or Sweet Soy Cream (page 4), divided

¼ cup agave syrup

¼ cup fresh blueberries, for garnish

4 sprigs fresh rosemary, for garnish

# Peppered Agave Figs (GF)

**Makes 4 servings**

1 tablespoon canola oil

¼ cup Basil Soy Ricotta
(page 8)

¼ cup agave syrup

½ teaspoon freshly ground
black pepper

12 large fresh figs

Fresh figs are fragile and seasonal; we find them in the markets only during those weeks in summer and early fall when they're actually on the trees. Because of this, a lot of people don't seem to know what to do with them, preferring the sturdier, ever-present dried version. Here I give their sweet, soft flesh a slight dash of spice and an extra nibble of protein. These would be great on a cheese plate.

---

Heat the oil in a medium skillet over medium-high heat. Add the ricotta and cook for 5 to 10 minutes, stirring occasionally, until it browns on the bottom and acquires a drier texture.

In a small bowl or measuring cup with a pouring spout, stir the agave syrup and pepper together.

Partially quarter each fig, starting at the stem end and stopping ½ inch before the bottom so that you have a reservoir to hold the filling. Gently press each fig open. Spoon 1 teaspoon of the cooked ricotta into the center of each. Arrange on plates or a pretty serving platter and drizzle the peppered agave syrup over the top.

# Everybody-Dives-In Chocolate Chip Brownies (SF/GF)

**Makes about 12 brownies**

¾ cup vegan buttery spread (such as Earth Balance brand), melted

4 ounces rice yogurt

1½ teaspoons vanilla extract

1¼ cups evaporated cane juice

1½ cups gluten-free all-purpose flour

½ cup unsweetened cocoa powder

1 teaspoon baking powder

¼ teaspoon baking soda

1 cup rice milk

1 cup vegan chocolate chips

Canola oil cooking spray

These brownies are one of our most popular desserts—because they're so rich and chocolaty, of course, but also because so many people can enjoy them regardless of food sensitivities. They're gluten-free, soy-free, and nut-free. And they're super either plain or dressed up into warm brownie sundaes with coconut milk ice cream and chocolaty syrup. This recipe originally came from my big sister, Afi Howell, an excellent vegan pastry chef. I adapted it to be gluten- and soy-free. Luckily, she likes them that way too.

---

Preheat the oven to 350 degrees F.

In the bowl of a stand mixer fitted with the whisk attachment (or substitute a hand mixer), combine the buttery spread, yogurt, vanilla, and cane juice. Whip until the mixture is thoroughly combined and slightly fluffy, about 5 minutes.

If you're using a stand mixer, combine the flour, cocoa, baking powder, and baking soda in a separate bowl while the wet ingredients are being whipped. If you're using a hand mixer, finish whipping the wet ingredients first, turn off the mixer, and then mix the dry ingredients in a separate bowl.

Add the dry ingredients to the wet ingredients, then add the milk and mix until thoroughly combined. Using a spatula, fold in the chocolate chips.

Coat a brownie pan (such as an 8-by-8-inch Pyrex) with the cooking spray and pour the batter into the pan. Bake until the brownies are firm in the center and a wooden toothpick inserted into the center has just a few crumbles sticking to it, 18 to 20 minutes.

# Strawberry Crepes with Custard Sauce (SF/GF)

Crepes sound intimidating, but this recipe couldn't be simpler. It was one of the first desserts I developed, although it could just as easily serve as a sweet breakfast. It tastes best when local strawberries are at the height of their season.

To make the strawberries, put the sliced strawberries in a medium bowl and toss with the cane and lemon juices. Make sure you do this step first so the berries have time to release some of their juices.

To make the custard, put the egg replacer and the hazelnut milk in a small bowl and whip with a whisk until frothy. Pour the mixture into a saucepan and cook over medium-low heat until it starts to thicken, 2 to 3 minutes. Add the cinnamon (or more to taste), maple syrup, and sugar, whisking until the mixture thickens and looks like a custard, about 5 to 7 minutes.

To make the crepes, whisk the milk and egg foam in a medium bowl, then add the buttery spread and whisk until combined. In a large bowl, whisk the flour, sugar, and confectioners' sugar. Add the wet ingredients to the dry ingredients and whisk until smooth.

If you'll be serving the crepes all at once, preheat the oven to 200 degrees F. Warm the crepes in a single layer on 2 large baking sheets until you're ready to serve.

Spray a small crepe pan or frying pan with the cooking spray and heat over medium heat. Using about ¼ cup of batter, coat the bottom of the pan with a thin layer of batter. Cook for about 1 minute, until the crepe starts to bubble in the middle and turns opaque. Loosen the edges with a soft spatula, then flip the crepe and cook for 1 minute more on the other side, until the edges are crisp while the middle is still soft. If you prefer a drier crepe, cook for 1 to 2 minutes longer. Remove the crepe, either to a plate or a baking sheet, and repeat with the remaining batter.

To serve, fold the crepes into a cup shape in bowls, or fold into a triangle shape on plates. Spoon a few tablespoons of rice cream on the bottom of the cup or over the triangle, divide the strawberries among the crepes, and spoon a tablespoon of custard over the strawberries.

**Makes a dozen 6-inch crepes**

For the strawberries:

1 cup strawberries, hulled and sliced ⅛-inch thick

1 tablespoon evaporated cane juice or agave syrup

2 teaspoons freshly squeezed lemon juice

For the custard:

1 tablespoon egg replacer (such as Ener-G brand)

1 cup hazelnut milk (such as Pacific brand), warmed

½ teaspoon ground cinnamon

1 tablespoon maple syrup

2 teaspoons sugar

For the crepes:

1⅓ cups unsweetened soy milk

⅓ cup Egg Foam (page 3)

2 tablespoons vegan buttery spread (such as Earth Balance brand), melted

1 cup gluten-free all-purpose flour

2 tablespoons sugar (optional)

¼ cup sifted confectioners' sugar

Canola oil cooking spray, for coating the pan

For garnish:

½ cup Sweet Rice Cream (page 8) or store-bought rice whipped cream (optional)

# Black Plum–Ginger Sorbet with Lemon Cream (SF/GF)

**Makes about 1 quart**

For the sorbet:

6 small black plums (about 1 pound), halved, pitted, and sliced

3 cardamom pods

½ cup evaporated cane juice

¾ cup water

¼ cup ginger brandy

For the lemon cream:

¼ cup packed fresh lemon verbena leaves

½ cup water

½ cup sugar

1 cup Sweet Rice Cream (page 8)

Ginger brandy gives this sorbet a grown-up touch, and leaving the skin on the plums adds some astringent balance to the summer sweetness. Make this recipe, which I adapted for vegan diets (and ginger fans) from the Kitchn (TheKitchn.com), a day or two ahead if you can to intensify the flavors. On warm nights at Plum, this cold and creamy combo is both lovely and refreshing, layered in clear glasses or glass bowls.

---

To make the sorbet, put the plums in a small saucepan, adding water to cover. Cook over medium heat, stirring occasionally, until the plums are soft but not turned to mush, about 15 minutes.

Using the back of a knife or a mortar and pestle, lightly bruise the cardamom pods. Combine the pods, the cane juice, and the water in another small saucepan and cook on a low simmer for a few minutes until the sugar dissolves. Stir in the ginger brandy. Remove from the heat and set aside to cool.

Puree the cooked plums in a blender or the bowl of a food processor until smooth. Add the sugar syrup and puree again. Strain the puree through a fine-mesh sieve and refrigerate in a covered container until thoroughly chilled—at least 4 to 6 hours, or preferably overnight.

Freeze the sorbet in an ice cream maker according to the manufacturer's instructions until it's just solid enough to scoop, about 15 minutes. If you won't be using it right away, transfer it to another container, place a layer of plastic wrap directly on top of the sorbet to seal it, cover the container, and store it in the freezer.

To make the lemon cream, using the back of a knife or a mortar and pestle, bruise the lemon verbena leaves and finely chop them. Combine the water and sugar in a small saucepan over low heat. Allow the mixture to come to a simmer for a few minutes, stirring occasionally to dissolve the sugar and create a simple syrup. Stir in the lemon verbena leaves and remove the pan from the heat. Steep the leaves for 10 to 15 minutes and then refrigerate the syrup. Strain out the leaves if you aren't going to use the syrup within a few hours.

Using a wooden spoon, hand mixer, or food processor, whip the rice cream with 1 tablespoon of lemon verbena syrup until it is fluffy, adding more syrup to taste. Don't use more than about 3 tablespoons, or the mixture will lose its loft.

Layer the sorbet and cream in clear glass dishes and serve.

# Fresh Blueberry Shortcake

**Makes 6 servings**

For the shortcake:

2 cups all-purpose flour, plus more for flouring the work surface

2½ teaspoons baking powder

½ teaspoon salt

⅓ cup vegan shortening (such as Earth Balance brand) or canola oil, plus more for greasing the baking sheet

¾ cup unsweetened soy milk

1 tablespoon vegan buttery spread (such as Earth Balance brand), softened

For the blueberry filling:

2 cups fresh blueberries

2 tablespoons agave syrup

1 tablespoon freshly squeezed lemon juice

For the blueberry sauce:

1 cup fresh blueberries, plus a handful for garnish

½ cup sugar

⅛ cup water

1½ tablespoons freshly squeezed lemon juice (from 1 medium lemon)

For garnish:

½ cup Sweet Soy Cream (page 4)

6 sprigs fresh mint

Biscuits are about as home-style as American food comes. Years ago I started working with a classic—the old-fashioned recipe right from the Clabber Girl baking powder can—adapting it with vegan ingredients to make my own version. These biscuits are just as flaky as the originals. As for turning them into shortcake, well—you always hear about strawberry shortcake, but Northwest native blueberries are prettier, more abundant, and easier to find in organic harvests. Put the two together for a juicy, saucy, new tradition.

---

Preheat the oven to 475 degrees F.

To make the shortcake, in a medium mixing bowl, stir together the flour, baking powder, and salt. Using a pastry blender or 2 forks, cut in the shortening until the mixture resembles coarse crumbs.

Make a well in the center of the mixture. Pour the milk all at once into the well. Using a fork, stir until the dough is just moistened and pulls away from the sides of the bowl (it will be sticky).

Flour a work surface. Using as light a touch as you can, pat the dough out with your hands to a ¾-inch thickness. Cut out circles with a 2½-inch biscuit cutter, dipping the cutter into flour between cutting each circle.

Lightly grease a baking sheet and place the biscuits close together on the sheet. Brush the tops with the buttery spread. Bake the biscuits until they're golden brown, 11 to 15 minutes. Remove from the oven and let cool.

To make the blueberry filling. In a medium bowl, gently toss the berries with the agave syrup and lemon juice. Set aside.

To make the blueberry sauce, put the berries, sugar, water, and lemon juice (or more juice to taste) in a medium saucepan. Cook over medium-high heat for 5 minutes, stirring occasionally, until some of the berries are broken but some remain whole.

To serve, when the biscuits have cooled slightly, halve each one. Put the bottom halves on 6 plates. Pour a few tablespoons of blueberry sauce on top, then a spoonful of cream and a few tablespoons of the blueberry filling. Add the top biscuit half, then drizzle a few more tablespoons of blueberry sauce and a spoonful of cream over all. Garnish with blueberries and a sprig of mint.

# Copper and Me

Copper is my first dog and I simply adore him. He's Plum's mascot and has made himself completely at home in our offices downstairs from the bistro.

Although he's an opportunistic omnivore, Copper loves homemade vegan food. He'd eat half a pound of fried tofu if I let him (I don't), so I make him his own special treats, from dog popsicles to smoky tofu jerky. Here's a great puppy food recipe that I mix with a vegan brand of kibble. I cook the yams in a pressure smoker, which gives them a super flavor, but if you don't have one, the method below works fine. Rice is also a great addition to this meal and useful if your pup has a sensitive tummy.

---

## Vegan Frankfurter and Smoked Yam Puppy Treats

Preheat the oven to 350 degrees F.

Slice the yam into ½-inch-thick rounds, leaving the skin on. Line a baking sheet or shallow, large baking pan with parchment paper and bake the yams for 20 to 30 minutes, until they are completely cooked through.

Chop the frankfurters into bite-size pieces appropriate for your dog. In a medium bowl, mix the cooked yam, frankfurters, tofu, oil, and water. If your dog prefers the consistency of canned dog food, blend the mixture in a food processor until it reaches the texture it likes.

**Makes 2 servings**

1 small red-skinned yam

2 store-bought vegan frankfurters (Copper likes the Field Roast brand)

4 ounces silken firm tofu, drained

1 tablespoon olive oil

¼ cup water

# Acknowledgments

It has taken a lot of people time, effort, and commitment to make this book possible. I would like to extend a humble thank-you to everyone who has taken the time to walk this path with me.

My deepest gratitude to both my parents for putting such faith in me, and thank-you to Afi Howell, my big sis, for supporting me, explaining my special brand of crazy to everyone, and making me desserts all the time, even though I don't pay her.

My true appreciation to Liz Dunn for seeing Plum's potential. My many thanks to Rebekah Denn for beautifully translating my words, to Charity Burggraaf for the lovely pictures, and to Aya Tiffany Sato for the beautiful author photo. Thank you to Elizabeth Rudge for the new cover photography and Jenn Elliot Blake for the prop styling. Susan Roxborough, my editor, I have met you many times before in life, and each time I learn something great. Thank you.

Thanks to Chef Wayne Johnson for being "my Chef," and teaching me at a quick glance the most important things I needed to know to run a kitchen. Thanks to Jim Graham, Bret Baba, and the whole Gram Baba crew for the beautiful design of the bistro. Thanks to Pan Kantiyavong (of Flower's Hardcore) for your beautiful, one-of-a-kind floral arrangements that help make Plum what it is.

My dinner party models and friends, Noreen Shinohara, Leann Crist, Ayna Miller, Nicole Lew, Andy Brown, Mika Sundberg, Gladys LY-AU Young, Ric Cochrane, Francesco Borghesi, and Hill Pierce, thank you for letting me steal you away from work for my book!

Thank you to all of my family and especially my aunties Doris Polston and Sharon Scott-Greene for being willing to be my recipe testers.

Give thanks to the farmers for the non-GMO food.

# Index

# Conversions

| VOLUME | | | LENGTH | | WEIGHT | |
|---|---|---|---|---|---|---|
| UNITED STATES | METRIC | IMPERIAL | UNITED STATES | METRIC | AVOIRDUPOIS | METRIC |
| ¼ tsp. | 1.25 mL | | ⅛ in. | 3 mm | ¼ oz. | 7 g |
| ½ tsp. | 2.5 mL | | ¼ in. | 6 mm | ½ oz. | 15 g |
| 1 tsp. | 5 mL | | ½ in. | 1.25 cm | 1 oz. | 30 g |
| ½ Tbsp. | 7.5 mL | | 1 in. | 2.5 cm | 2 oz. | 60 g |
| 1 Tbsp. | 15 mL | | 1 ft. | 30 cm | 3 oz. | 90 g |
| ⅛ c. | 30 mL | 1 fl. oz. | | | 4 oz. | 115 g |
| ¼ c. | 60 mL | 2 fl. oz. | | | 5 oz. | 150 g |
| ⅓ c. | 80 mL | 2.5 fl. oz. | | | 6 oz. | 175 g |
| ½ c. | 120 mL | 4 fl. oz. | | | 7 oz. | 200 g |
| 1 c. | 230 mL | 8 fl. oz. | | | 8 oz. (½ lb.) | 225 g |
| 2 c. (1 pt.) | 460 mL | 16 fl. oz. | | | 9 oz. | 250 g |
| 1 qt. | 1 L | 32 fl. oz. | | | 10 oz. | 300 g |

## TEMPERATURE

| OVEN MARK | FAHREN-HEIT | CELSIUS | GAS | | AVOIRDUPOIS | METRIC |
|---|---|---|---|---|---|---|
| | | | | | 11 oz. | 325 g |
| | | | | | 12 oz. | 350 g |
| Very cool | 250–275 | 120–135 | ½–1 | | 13 oz. | 375 g |
| Cool | 300 | 150 | 2 | | 14 oz. | 400 g |
| Warm | 325 | 165 | 3 | | 15 oz. | 425 g |
| Moderate | 350 | 175 | 4 | | 16 oz. (1 lb.) | 450 g |
| Moderately hot | 375 | 190 | 5 | | 1½ lb. | 750 g |
| Fairly hot | 400 | 200 | 6 | | 2 lb. | 900 g |
| Hot | 425 | 220 | 7 | | 2¼ lb. | 1 kg |
| Very hot | 450 | 230 | 8 | | 3 lb. | 1.4 kg |
| Very hot | 475 | 245 | 9 | | 4 lb. | 1.8 kg |

For ease of use, conversions have been rounded.